CW00643822

a clwyd anthology

FOR JOHN DAVIES OF PRESTATYN
AND KEVERNE SMITH OF WREXHAM

a clwyd anthology

edited by Dewi Roberts

seren

seren is the book imprint of
Poetry Wales Press Ltd
Wyndham Street, Bridgend, Mid Glamorgan

A CIP record for this title is available from
the British Library CIP Office

ISBN 1-85411-144-2

The publisher acknowledges the financial support of the Arts Council of Wales

Cover painting:
'Vale of Llangollen from Corwen, Winter 1995'
by Peter Prendergast

Printed by The Cromwell Press Ltd
Melksham

Contents

11 Introduction

Topography

17 Anon: *The Seven Wonders of Wales*
17 William Hazlitt: *A Walk Through the Dee Valley*
18 John Idris Jones: *An Old Lady*
20 Emlyn Williams: *Africa?*
21 Richard Brinsley Sheridan: *A Curse on Mold*
21 Dorothy Hartley: *Living on a Mountain*
22 A.A. Gill: *Bilingualism*
23 Edmund Crispin: *The Mold Clue*
23 John Jones: *My Native Town*
24 W.E. Griffiths: *The Border*
25 Harriet Hemans: *Felicia Hemans at St Asaph*
26 John Davies: *Farmland*
27 John Williams: *Excavating the Clwydian Hills*
27 Gerard Manley Hopkins: *A Letter from St Beuno's*
28 Daniel Defoe: *A Fine Prospect*
28 Glenda Beagan: *A Walk Through Darkness*
30 Ellis Peters: *Gwytherin*
32 Joseph Hucks: *A View of the Clwyd*
32 Samuel Johnson: *Dyserth Waterfall*
33 Anon: *At Variance*
33 Gerard Manley Hopkins: *An Instress and Charm*
34 Gerard Manley Hopkins: *Hurrahing in Harvest*
34 W.T. Palmer: *Elwy and Clwyd*
36 Glenda Beagan: *Shaman*
37 Gerard Manley Hopkins: *In the Valley of the Elwy*
38 Lord Devenport: *The House on the Moors*
39 Wilson MacArthur: *Gwylfa Hiraethog*
40 Alun Llewellyn-Williams: *A Trip to Llety'r Eos*
41 Peter Marshall: *Cerrigydruddion*
42 Sue Trevelyan-Jones: *Coastal Erosion*
43 George Porter: *A Victorian Hotel*
45 H.V. Morton: *This Stretch of Lovely Coast*
46 Adrian Henri: *Rhyl Sands*
46 Harry Thomas: *Venice in Wales*

48 Bryan Asden: *Today*
49 Charles Kingsley: *The Sands of Dee*
49 Leslie Brockbank: *Wildfowling on the Welsh Side*
50 Michael Drayton: *The All-Knowing Dee*
51 John Rhys: *The Divinity of the Dee*
51 Gladys Mary Coles: *Wet Spring Bank Holiday, Dee Estuary*
52 Emyr Humphreys: *An Estuary View*
53 John Richards: *Shotton*
54 John Davies: *New spaces, Clwyd*
55 Raymond Edwards: *Rhosllanerchrugog*
56 Oliver Onions: *A Winter Journey*
57 A.G. Prys-Jones: *At Valle Crucis*
58 Anon: *Llangollen Ale*
59 Jan Morris: *A Wonder of the Age*
60 Merlin Waterson: *Erddig Restored*
61 Daniel Owen: *A Lover of Nature*

People

65 Evelyn Waugh: *Many Miles Astray*
65 Beatrix Potter: *The Welsh Type*
66 Evelyn Waugh: *The Llanaba Silver Band*
68 Gutun Owain: *Asking a Stallion*
70 John Cowper Powys: *Mystic Enchantment*
70 A.G. Bradley: *Katherine of Berain*
72 John Parry: *Humphrey Llwyd*
73 Lord Herbert of Cherbury: *Self Restraint*
74 H.B. Irving: *The Welshness of Judge Jeffreys*
75 Augustus John: *The Gypsy Girl*
76 John Ceiriog Hughes: *A Bushel of Chaff*
77 Sir Leonard Twiston-Davies & Averyl Edwards: *Twm O'r Nant*
79 Richard Warner: *A Visit to Pennant*
80 John Davies: *Downing*
81 A.H. Dodd: *The Williams Wynns*
82 Emyr Humphreys: *Pastoral*
83 David Jones: *An Indelible Mark on the Soul*
85 'Nimrod' (Charles James Apperley): *Three Colourful Characters*
87 Robert Graves: *Dirty Williams*
87 T. Gwynn Jones: *Rural Poverty*
88 Nathaniel Hawthorne: *An American Eavesdropper*
89 Sir Henry Morton Stanley: *Early Memories*

91 Nathaniel Hawthorne: *A Surprise Visit*
92 Rhoda Broughton: *A Dull Watering-Place*
93 Francis Kilvert: *Kilvert at Llangollen*
94 James Gibson Lockhart: *Scott Visits the Ladies*
95 J. Vyrnwy Morgan: *Thomas Gee*
97 Ronnie Knox-Mawer: *The Ecclesiastical Tour*
99 Askew Roberts: *Henry M. Stanley*
99 John Lloyd: *Hiraeth*
100 Wynford Vaughan Thomas: *Edward Lloyd and Perpetual Motion*
101 Washington Irving: *The One-Legged Fisherman*
103 Natheniel Hawthorne: *The Ill-Fated Launch*
105 Daniel Owen: *Mr Phillips*
106 John Ceiriog Hughes: *A Pothersome Pair*
107 Wilfred Owen: *A Poet's Juvenilia*
108 Anon: *Three Hinds of Denbighshire*
109 George Cornwallis West: *Old Hughes of Kinmel*
110 Emlyn Williams: *An Urban Impact*
111 T.E. Ellis: *Commemoration*
112 T. Gwynn Jones: *The Privilege*
114 Hugh Evans: *A World Beyond*
115 Adam Mars-Jones: *Philip Yorke,The Last Squire of Erddig*
117 Emlyn Williams: *The Scholarship Boy*
118 Robert Graves: *Thinking of the Dead*
119 John Moore: *The Elusive Steak*
120 H.G. Wells: *Jones*
122 Philip Rock: *Drowning in Wales*
122 Emyr Humphreys: *County School Pride*
123 George Melly: *Fishing on the Clwyd*
124 Caradoc Pritchard: *Inside Denbigh Asylum*
127 Dewi Roberts: *Mrs Darby*
129 Emyr Humphreys: *Twenty-four Pairs of Socks*
130 Euros Bowen: *Saliwt*

History

135 Gladys Mary Coles: *Pontnewydd Cave, Valley of the Elwy*
135 Frances Lynch: *The Bronze Age in Denbighshire*
137 John Speede: *The Ordouices*
137 W. Watkin Davies: *Bangor Iscoed*
138 Thomas Pennant: *Owain Glyndwr at Sycharth*
141 Iolo Goch: *Glyndwr's Home*

143 T.E. Ellis: *An Enduring Heritage*
143 Lewis Glyn Cothi: *The Saxons of Flint*
145 S. Baring Gould: *The Elwy Valley*
146 Gwyn Williams: *A Plea to Sir Bribem*
147 Richard Warner: *The Perils of Mining*
148 David Jones: *The High Price of Corn*
149 Harry Tobit Evans: *Sister Rebecca*
149 George G. Lerry: *The Battle of Cinder Hill*
151 Askew Roberts: *The Coastal Line*
151 Roderick O'Flanagan: *A Railway Catastrophe*
152 A *Times* Correspondent: *Troubled Times*
154 Trevor Herbert: *Dispute and Conflict*
155 *Y Genedl Cymreig*: *A Tithe Riot*
156 Stowers Johnson: *Explosive Times*
156 Anon: *A Wartime Escape*
157 Terence Doyle: *Casualties of Peace*
159 Tim Liardet: *Stigmata*
161 Anon: *The Gresford Disaster*
163 I.D. Hooson: *The Grinding*
163 Dewi Humphries: *VE Day*
164 Gladys Mary Coles: *The Dornier*
166 *The Denbighshire Free Press*: *Nature Defeating Man*
166 Ian Chesterman: *The Men Who Make The Steel*
167 Steve Griffiths: *Misrule,Towyn 1990*

Culture and Religion

173 Dylan Thomas: *At the Eisteddfod*
175 Raymond Edwards: *A Village of Colliers*
175 John Ceiriog Hughes: *What Passes and Endures*
176 Gwyn Williams: *The Caerwys Eisteddfod*
177 A.S. Vaughan Thomas: *Hugh Holland*
178 Donald Moore: *Artists in Clwyd*
180 Samuel Johnson: *An After Dinner Discourse*
180 Cecil Price: *Gaining Cheap Admittance*
181 A.H. Dodd: *A Theatre-goer With a Cloven Hoof*
182 T.M. Haydn Rees: *Theatre Clwyd*
183 David Bell: *Richard Wilson*
184 Felix Mendelssohn : *'Dreadful, Vulgar, Out-of-tune Trash...'*
184 Michael Faraday: *The Musical 'Boots'*
185 Raymond Renowden: *Music in the Cathedral*

186 Robert Roberts: *A Scholar's Early Life*
187 Derek Llwyd Morgan: *Ferocious Honesty*
188 Kate Roberts: *Reflections*
188 Kate Roberts: *Struggle*
188 Euros Bowen: *Bits and Pieces*
189 R.S. Thomas: *Llanrhaeadr-ym-Mochnant*
190 Gerard Manley Hopkins: *St Winefride's Well*
191 Celia Fiennes: *Blind Zeale*
191 Philip Metcalf: *A Complete and Miraculous Cure*
193 John Cowper Powys: *Eliseg*
193 William Roscoe: *A Well Preserved Corpse*
194 C.R. Williams: *The Problems of Flintshire Priests*
195 S. Baring Gould: *Ffynnon Fair*
195 William Williams: *Persecution*
196 J.J. Morgan: *Revivalism*
198 Daniel Owen: *Principles of Government*
199 Emyr Humphreys: *Chapel-going in Winter*
200 John Wesley: *Wesley in Mold*
200 Dennis Griffiths: *Religious Awakening in Buckley*

Folklore

205 Henry Morton Stanley: *Witches, Ghosts, Fairies, Ghosts*
206 A.G. Bradley: *The Conjuror's Revenge*
208 Gerard Manley Hopkins: *Miss Jones and the Kippernappers*
208 W. Bezant Lowe: *The Ghost of Pribwll*
209 W.T. Palmer: *Saint George in Clwyd*
210 J.O. Halliwell: *The Tan-yr-Ogo Witch*
210 Jan Morris: *A Notorious Well*
211 Marie Trevelyan: *An Ingenious Way to Kill Dragons*
212 W.T. Palmer: *Sir John and the Dragon*
212 A.G. Bradley: *Sir Richard and 'The Evil One'*
213 Elias Owen: *May Eve and May Day Customs*
214 Ken Radford: *The Widow of Penley*
216 Anon: *A Welsh Robin Hood*
218 Frederick J. Harris: *Visitations of Death*
218 Robert Parry: *Death and the Spirits*

219 *Acknowledgements*

Introduction

In this book the reader will find a mixture of the old and the new, fact and fiction, provocation and celebration.

Much has been written over the years about Clwyd in its many facets but this anthology represents the first attempt to present a selection of this material. Inevitably there is a strong emphasis on the history of the region. We find the poet Gladys Mary Coles writing of the earliest recorded human life in the region; Thomas Pennant describing Owain Glyndwr's home at Sycharth; the eighteenth century travel writer Richard Warner describing the mining conditions of the period; a schoolboy recalling V.E. day in the Wrexham area; the lyricist Ian Chesterman lamenting the demise of British steelmaking at Shotton; and, bringing us into our own decade, Steve Griffiths evoking the terror of the Towyn floods.

But what of the geographical focus of the book? The Vale of Clwyd can be clearly seen as one of two significant areas of the county. "...In its way there can hardly be anything to beat the Vale of Clwyd," wrote Gerard Manley Hopkins soon after his arrival in North Wales in 1874 to take up his studies for the Jesuit priesthood. Having lived in the valley throughout my life I share his enthusiastic sentiment.

Denbigh and Ruthin are the neighbouring towns in the valley, which is guarded to the north-east by the Clwydian hills, the famous Moel Fammau being the highest of these. Denbigh, the former county town of Denbighshire, has a strong literary heritage. The oldest publishing company in Wales was established here by the liberal reformer Thomas Gee in 1845, and in the nineteen-thirties was run by the novelist Kate Roberts and her husband. She disliked certain aspects of life in the town and regretted the poor quality of spoken Welsh.

When Beatrix Potter visited the area she claimed that the people were "deteriorated by much inbreeding", an extreme colonial attitude shared with Evelyn Waugh's Dr Fagan: "Their sons and daughters rarely mate with human kind except their own". Nathaniel Hawthorne was none too complimentary about the women of Ruthin, describing them as "witch-like . . . very unlike anything feminine in America".

The county's other focal point is the Dee valley, which has been a mecca for writers and artists for over two centuries. "O Sylvan Dee

... the river of Paradise, where I will drink of the waters of life," exclaimed an ecstatic Hazlitt.

Llangollen, of course, plays a unique role culturally as the annual venue for the International Eisteddfod. "What a rush of dancing Llangollen feet," observed Dylan Thomas. By a stroke of irony, in the nineteenth century Felix Mendelssohn unleashed a torrent of abuse on hearing a Llangollen harpist play: he complained of "dreadful, vulgar, out-of-tune trash".

To the south of the Dee valley lie the Berwyn hills which extend, mile after mile, into Powys. Almost directly on the county boundary is the village of Llanrhaeadr-ym-Mochnant, a fairly unremarkable little place, one might think, until one recalls that this was where William Morgan translated the Bible into Welsh.

...The smooth words
Over which his mind flowed
Have become an heirloom

writes R.S. Thomas.

Isolated but not conventionally attractive places appeal to me, partly because they tend to be off the tourist map. Alun Llewelyn-Williams writes of "the pallid heavens of Hiraethog" and this seems an apt description. On walks over the moorland one may discover the moss-covered remnants of nineteenth century shepherds' huts, and the area is still important in terms of sheep farming. Hiraethog once stimulated a rich peasant tradition of poetry and song, and this concept of ordinary people making art out of where they are and what they are is now an area of academic interest. The shepherd-poet played an important double role in his rural circle.

But what of urban Clwyd? Wrexham is the largest town in Clwyd and has the definite atmosphere of a border community. St Giles' church is one of the seven wonders of Wales, and has an important American link, for Elihu Yale, who donated money to the college in Connecticut which bears his name, is buried here. Several villages have evolved within a few miles of Wrexham, notably Rhosllanerchrugog, which some would argue has itself assumed the size of a town. Described by Raymond Edwards as a "tribal community", it is the birthplace of many talented people; the actor Meredith Edwards among them

In his novels Emyr Humphreys has directed the literary spotlight on to Flintshire for English readers, while Emlyn Williams has revealed the same area through very different eyes. Flint itself is now a part of the Deeside conurbation, which also includes Connah's Quay and Queensferry. It is an intensely anglicized area and, in comparison with many places at the heart of the county, seems quite un-Welsh. "If once again I venture there / May death a second visit spare" wrote Lewis Glyn Cothi following a visit to a wedding feast at Flint.

Mold, the present administrative centre of the county, has strong associations with Daniel Owen, who is frequently referred to as the 'Welsh Dickens'. Many agree that he is without equal in Welsh literature, being an acute observer of human character. Theatre Clwyd, which stands in a rural setting on the edge of Mold, has assumed a vital role in the cultural life of Wales since it opened in 1976. It has staged major productions with actors of international repute, including Vanessa Redgrave and Sir Anthony Hopkins.

In this introduction it has only been possible to refer to a few of the many items included, and the reader will quickly discover those of greatest personal interest. In an early inclusion in the book John Idris Jones, writing in 1968, refers to the bureaucratic decision to take from the old county of Denbighshire, "the old lady" as he affectionately describes it, "her final virtue of autonomy in local government"; and so Clwyd, which had previously incorporated both Denbighshire and Flintshire, replaced them in 1974. But since then further changes have been announced and at the time of writing these are imminent.

This seems an opportune time, therefore, in which to record Clwyd's literary heritage, which celebrates the culture, history, people and landscape of this unique corner of Wales.

Dewi Roberts, Denbigh

I am indebted to Clwyd Library Service for launching this book during their 1995 Library Festival.

Warm thanks are also due to Mick Felton, of Seren, who has made working with a publisher such a stimulating experience, and John Davies for the encouraging letters which he sent me while I was working on the anthology.

D.R.

Topography

The Seven Wonders of Wales
Anon.

Pistyll Rhaeadr and Wrexham steeple,
Snowdon's mountain without its people,
Overton yew trees, Gresford bells,
Llangollen bridge and St Winifred's well.

A Walk Through the Dee Valley
William Hazlitt

It was on the 10th of April 1790 that I sat down to a volume of the 'New Eloise,' at the inn at Llangollen, over a bottle of sherry and a cold chicken. The letter I chose was that in which St. Preux describes his feelings as he first caught a glimpse from the heights of the Jura of the Pays de Vaud, which I had brought with me as a *bon bouche* to crown the evening with. It was my birthday, and I had for the first time come from a place in the neighbourhood to visit this delightful spot. The road to Llangollen turns off between Chirk and Wrexham; and on passing a certain point you come all at once upon the valley, which opens like an amphitheatre, broad, barren hills rising in majestic state on either side, with 'green upland swells that echo to the bleat of flocks' below, and the river Dee babbling over its stony bed in the midst of them. The valley at this time 'glittered green with sunny showers,' and a budding ash-tree dipped its tender branches in the chiding stream. How proud, how glad I was to walk along the highroad that overlooks the delicious prospect, repeating the lines which I have just quoted from Mr. Coleridge's poems! But besides the prospect which opened beneath my feet, another also opened to my inward sight, a heavenly vision, on which were written, in letters large as Hope could make them, these four words, LIBERTY, GENIUS, LOVE, VIRTUE, which have since faded into the light of common day, or mock my idle gaze.

> The beautiful is vanished and returns not.

Still, I would return some time or other to this enchanted spot, but I would return to it alone. What other self could I find to share that influx of thoughts, of regret, and delight, the fragments of which I could hardly conjure up to myself, so much have they been broken and defaced? I could stand on some tall rock, and overlook the precipice of years that separates me from what I then was. I was at that time going shortly to visit the poet whom I have above named. Where is he now? Not only I myself have changed; the world, which was then new to me, has become old and incorrigible. Yet will I turn to thee in thought, O sylvan Dee, in joy, in youth and gladness as thou then wert; and thou shalt always be to me the river of Paradise, where I will drink of the waters of life freely!

from *On Going on a Journey* (1817)

An Old Lady
John Idris Jones

Denbighshire is my home county, the county of my birth, but only just. Give or take a few hundred yards and the mewling infant would have dropped into Montgomeryshire, and as a result the edicts of officialdom and efficiency would have appended a Mont. rather than a Denbs. on all those papers which follow me around from one part of the globe to another. These labels and forms tell you where you've come from and where you are going to, and you carry the county of your birth around with you along with your baggage. Like on that sunny day when I drove over the bridge into Canada at Niagara Falls and stopped by the row of booths. The man in uniform asked me if I was an American citizen, got a negative answer, and then asked me where I was born, and I said very clearly, 'Llanrhaiadr Ym Mochnant, Denbighshire.' He asked me if that was in England and I said 'Yes' (for simplicity's sake) and he got rid of me quickly.

One really interesting geographical fact about this county is that it looks like the head of an old woman. She is bent, slightly crazed, looking eastwards. She has a turned-up pixie nose and her mouth is half open. She is old, worn, defeated, but she is cocking a snook both at the English who have ravaged her for centuries and at the Boundaries Commission who have made Proposals to her and got no answer and who are set to take from her her final virtue of autonomy in local government. The lines of her face are strung along the bumpy contours of the Clwyd Hills (which are outside my window as I write). These hills — Moel Famau, at 1,820 feet above sea level is the tallest — are the last barrier between Wales and England and comprise that first small step which the marauder or tourist takes as he treks westwards looking for the real Wales to fight or photograph. But even though the old woman's virtue is long gone, she knows her place, which is to defend to the death the counties of Merioneth, Caernarfon and — bless her most pure and hallowed maternal Welshness — Anglesey, in which the cinders of real Welshness are still smouldering, and to turn the most offensive phrase and face towards the bourgeois Englishness of Cheshire, the well-bred snobbery of Shropshire, and the hideous ugliness of industrial Merseyside. Denbighshire knows where she lies: her allegiances, beneath the soil which through centuries has been much trampled upon, are still there.

Llanrhaiadr Ym Mochnant sits on her right shoulder, straddling the border between the counties of Denbigh and Montgomery. Over the Berwyn Hills, in the direction taken by George Borrow, complaining all the way about the beer, is Merioneth. And behind you is Montgomery. Both of them in my childhood seemed bleak and lonely counties, full of moors, cold winds, sheep, winding roads that seemed to go nowhere, signposts pointing in one direction only and farms made of stones. At week-ends, when the petrol rationing allowed, we used to drive westwards to see my grandparents at Borthygest, near Portmadoc and the trip took us out of Denbighshire and over the Berwyns, along an unfenced road with deep ditches and between huge rocks and yellowing mountain grass, to that capital of all that's bleak, Bala, and then on westwards to the softer area where the sea was.

I cannot write about Denbighshire in geographical terms. I can only see the place through the filter of my own perceptions and therefore in terms of my exposure to the county in my childhood, youth and adulthood. She has followed my growth with interest. Always in the background, behind my shoulder, there have been those hills and those green fields: from the lonely community where I was born to the rich acres of the Clwyd Valley, that most well-bred place, where I was well bred.

To present the place in external terms is possible, but superficial. A county, like every person, has a soul. She has a reality, an inner self with a rhythm and life of her own, apart from the world of appearances. Apart from personality, she has character. And character is a hard word; a word for something underneath which is immutable.

That is why I cannot present her as a series of pictures, of coloured snapshots. I do not want to degrade the county to a mere list of nicely decorated places, presented with the soulless ubiquity of the American Viewmaster, which gives you pictures in 3D even. Photography is not conducive to reality. The pictures in the mind which are painted for us by our own unique experience are infused with our humanity- the relationship between the mind and its environment, especially the environment of childhood and home, is a love affair which tests all other love affairs; it is the touchstone of all we feel to be real, good and worthwhile: it is the curtain against which we play the drama of our lives.

Denbighshire, old lady, you are all things to all men. Within the boundaries of your personality you have highland and lowland, industries and moors, offices and farms, the Welsh and the English, land and sea. But down your centre you have the Clwyd Valley, that most refined of valleys. And though Woman is fickle, and life is precarious, that valley which marks your countenance remains constantly a receptacle of the deeper qualities of Welsh culture which are your heritage and true self. And when I roam over the places I have seen, and reflect upon the scenes I have yet to observe, I can conceive of no thing more beautiful and more lasting than the quality of the light which bathes the Clwyd hills as the sun is setting in the West.

from *The Anglo-Welsh Review* (1968)

Africa?
Emlyn Williams

A large slate-roofed, whitewashed box perched on a hillock, not attractive, not ugly, our house dominated Glanrafon, which must be the easiest less-than-a-village in the world to describe: it contained, in a green and shallow hollow, a row of fourteen stone cottages. Across the road from them, the 'river' — trickling water three feet wide and two inches deep except when in flood, when it was six.

From our house, on every hand around the village there rose a gentle swell: to the left, the swell of field up to the woods, and to the right, behind the cottages, the swell of back-gardens (each with its pigsty) up to a protective ridge. Straight ahead the road, after dipping from us and crossing a lane, skirted the gamekeeper's cottage on the edge of the wooded Gyrn Castle estate, swelled up on the other side, past Parry's farm and the pump, and disappeared between trees up to Llanasa, the village whose parish we were in. Our own village lay so sheltered that it was hard to believe that the white specks scattered sometimes on the green slope of the field were not flowers until they soared, all together marvellously, and turned into seagulls. Far out of sight were the blue-grey stretches of the estuary with, half in sky and half in sea, small yachts like icebergs. From the height beyond our house, a field away, you could see across to the Cheshire plain; and once, sitting with my father in the cart on his way down to Mostyn for beer, I asked him what the place was over the water, with all that sand? He said it was another country, where Welsh was not spoken and the public-houses were open on Sunday. I remembered the Sahara and asked if it was Africa. He laughed and said it was.

from *George* (1961)

A Curse on Mold
Richard Brinsley Sheridan

Were I to curse the man I hate,
From youth till I grow old,
Oh! might he be condemned by fate
To waste his days in Mold.

Living on a Mountain
Dorothy Hartley

It is difficult to write of British mountains when living on one, and our small village is crouched like a rock rabbit on the sloping edge of a mountain . . . it's like criticising one's own grandfather.

The wall stones of our house are cut from the quarry behind, the slates overhead are from Glyndyfrdwy old quarries (where the great forty-feet water wheel now stands moss grown and idle). The little wall that holds us from slipping off the mountain into the river is built of water-worn fossil rocks, from the bed that gurgles past Ty-issa.

Half the larder floor *is* rock, living rock still in the mountain, and they have had to shape the side wall to fit over it. No, the mountain, to one that lives on *the* mountain, is a part of himself, inseparable from his existence. Though you may be bed-ridden indoors, and never set foot outside for weeks, you feel the mountain there, reminding you of its presence day and night. The whiff of peat, wavering from the hearth, drifts like smoke through the senses, all day long, and suddenly there comes the howl and cry of the wind, tearing down from the heights to fling itself against your door, or to lift and lie down with a shudder under your carpet. The queer distinct smell that comes down in the wet weather . . . the sense of a larger presence, always above you, even when thick mist and fog settle down close, and you see no farther than the gate for weeks, make you *feel* the mountain there, always.

from *The Countryman's England* (1935)

Bilingualism

A.A. Gill

As you drive through north Wales the sign posts sing to you in two part harmony, the names of places are evocative. Heavy and poignant, the very sounds of this ancient language, rooted in this majestic landscape, seem to summon up all the generosity, warmth and kindness for which the Welsh are famous: Rhyl, Mold, Flint.

God I have problems with the Welsh. Every bloody sign is written in English and Welsh, so that the sign for Flint, a town that only a man driving a crane with a demolition ball attached would visit with a smile, is spelt as Fflint and Flint. They are absurd. Flint, so ghastly they had to name it twice. The only writing on the streets that is solely in English is the graffiti sprayed everywhere by the Sons Of Glendower, the Postmen Pat of the international brotherhood of terrorists: 'English piss off home and take Max Boyce with you.'

The Sunday Times, 31 October 1993

The Mold Clue
Edmund Crispin

'Well,' said Cadogan, 'I don't see how this helps.' He read the advertisement aloud: 'Ryde, Leeds, West, Mold, Berlin. Aaron Rosseter, Solicitor, 139A Cornmarket. Well, what are we to conclude from that ?'

'I don't exactly know,' said Fen. 'And yet I feel somehow I ought to. Holmes would have made mincemeat of it — he was good on agony columns. Mold, Mold. What is Mold anyway?' He went to the encyclopaedia and took out a volume. After a moments search: '"Urban district and market town of Flintshire. Thirteen miles from Chester . . . centre of important lead and coal mines . . . brick, nails, beer, etc . . ." Does that convey anything to you?'

'Nothing at all . . .'

'Well, that may be,' Fen restored the book to its place. 'But if so, it's a remarkable collection. Mold. Mold,' he added in tones of faint reproof.

from *The Moving Toyshop* (1946)

My Native Town
John Jones

Now slowly winding from the mountain's head,
Deep pits I witness, where the ore of lead
Is raised by miners from the stubborn soil,
To be transformed to various things by toil . . .
Industry's children are the sons of Wales,
No real starvation through their land prevails:
Their hills, though sterile, and their portion scant
They ask no affluence and they know no want;
No bounds they crave for but their native sod,
With leave to labour and to worship God.
Yet will they not oppression bear too long,
But burst their fetters — a resistless throng,
And prove that spirit not extinguished quite
Which shone conspicuous on the fields of fight,
And thinned the ranks of Saxons and of Danes

When thronging down they poured on British plains.
  From yon high prospect now I've ventured down
And stand delighted in my native town;
But whence the noises that assail mine ear?
What crowds before me with their goods appear?
'Tis market day — loud dealers strain their lungs
And High Street echoes with two different tongues:
The Welsh and English there alternate cry
'Rhai'n, rhai'n, yw pethau rhad' — 'Come buy, come buy!'
Now strangers hail raw natives as they meet,
Who cry 'Dim Saesneg', wanting power to greet.
Some few with signs their various bargains end,
Some curse the tongue they cannot comprehend.
But such as landlords more perfection reach —
They know each language and converse in each:
What should be foreign they pronounce quite well —
Scarce aught were better save the drink they sell.

(John Jones (1788-1858), known as 'Poet Jones' was one of the very few indigenous poets writing in English about North Wales in the nineteenth century. His 'native town' was Holywell.)

The Border

W.E. Griffiths

From rooftop level in Wrexham one's westward gaze roams over huddled villages and old colliery workings to the unobtrusive curve of purple moor above Minera. Eastward the foreground falls softly in wooded and pastured folds to the silent twisting Dee, beyond which nothing breaks the monotony till the sandstone hills of Bickerton and Peckforton like sleeping giants above the plain. The world thus embraced ranges between extremes of topography, geology, vegetation and human settlement. It is in fact two worlds — the world of the empty moors, the dark sentinels of the Welsh hills; and the world of the rich and wooded lowlands the English plain. Between the two lies Wrexham, a true border town.

But it is important to remember that the border has an infinitely longer history than the town. The border has always been a border, geographically, geologically, botanically and racially. Throughout prehistoric as well as historic times, its presence can be felt, its influence on settler and invader assessed. But in early times the site of the town was of no consequence. We look in vain here for the summer camps of Palaeolithic hunters, or the clearings of the first farmers; no Bronze Age necropolis or Iron Age *oppidum* sprang up on the banks of the Gwenfro. The local topography lacked these essentials which operate universally in the choice of primitive settlement. Here were no caves for shelter against the cold of the retreating ice — no fordable river, rich in fish; no open land, easy of tillage by digging- stick or foot-plough; no commanding hill for Iron Age camp or Roman fort. Hence a prehistory of Wrexham is a record of silence, a blank on the map.

from 'A History of Wrexham' (1977)

Felicia Hemans at St Asaph

Harriet Hemans

Those who only know the neighbourhood of St Asaph, from travelling along its highways, can be little aware how much delightful scenery is attainable, within walks of two or three miles distance from Mrs Hemans's residence. The placid beauty of the Clwyd, and the wilder graces of its sister stream, the Elwy, particularly in the vicinity of 'Our Lady's Well', and the interesting rocks and caves at Cefn, are little known to general tourists; though, by the lovers of her poetry, it will be remembered how sweetly she apostrophised the

> Fount of the chapel, with ages grey;

and how tenderly, amidst far different scenes, her thoughts reverted to the

> Cambrian river, with slow music gliding
> By pastoral hills, old woods, and ruined towers

from *The Works of Mrs Hemans*, with a memoir by her sister (1829)

Farmland

John Davies

Inland from the English-speaking sea,
where I lose my bearings and my wife translates,
market towns gather villages.
Henllan, Trefnant, Llanrhaeadr had come
past trees brushing mist from the fields
to Denbigh's plantation of telegraph poles.
Steps stood up, and high arched doors
checking again familiar faces
narrowly took me in. On her aunt's
coffin, flowers had drained the light
but not those packed pews: murmurs, ripples
were refilling farmland's hollows.

The minister's shock of eyebrows
hedging raw cheeks, he'd have hauled a ram.
Speech shook me off. It was tenors
gliding on familiar foreign words in search
of thermals drew me towards the woman
gone, to Joe who doesn't speak Welsh

or often, relying on closed ranks.
Once connection tunes its instruments,
feeling's airborne over fact
and, soaring, forgets it still bears
language asserting difference, how else
leap snags of common ground?

At the coast were fingers of cloud
all bruises and gold rings. Caravans
made one thin road an anywhere.
What we travel from also moves from us,
and gulls guarding clutches of pebbles
turned into people briefly then flew off.

from *Flight Patterns* (1991)

Excavating the Clwydian Hills
John Williams

On the east, the Vale of Clwyd is bounded by a chain of hills, the natural barrier of this part of Wales, running north and south, the summits of which command a very extensive view; on the one side into Lancashire and Cheshire and on the other the interior Alpine country of Caernarvonshire and Merioneth. On these hills are found no less than six primeval encampments, some of considerable size, originally occupied by the Britons, but afterwards occupied by the Romans. Four or five years since, a party of antiquarians commenced a series of diggings and found several stone arrowheads, knives, and other instruments of the early Britons; and fragments of Roman pottery. Previously a great number of gold and silver coins, bearing the inscription of the Roman emperors had been discovered on these mountains. The chain of the Clwydian Hills culminates in the lofty Moel Vamma, crowned with the Jubilee Tower, a building in the Egyptian style of architecture, raised in commemoration of George III attaining the fiftieth year of his reign. This conspicuous object stands at an elevation of nearly 2,000 feet above the level of the sea, and in Summer is the favourite resort of picnic parties.

from *Ancient and Modern Denbigh* (1856)

A Letter from St Beuno's
Gerard M. Hopkins

St. Beuno's, St. Asaph, North Wales. [29 August 1874]

My dearest Father,

I came here yesterday, to begin my studies in theology. I had expected to have another year's teaching at Roehampton, but now my ordination and profession will be earlier. The house stands on a steep hillside, it commands the long-drawn valley of the Clwyd to the sea, a vast prospect, and opposite is Snowdon and its range, just now it being bright visible but coming and going with the weather. The air seems to me very fresh and wholesome. Holidays till the 2nd of October. After that hours of study very close — lectures in dogmatic theology, moral ditto, canon law, church history, scripture, Hebrew and what not. I have half a mind to get up a little Welsh: all the neighbours speak it. I have said nothing about the house. It is built of limestone, decent outside, skimpin within, Gothic, like Lancing College done worse. The staircases, galleries, and bopeeps are inexpressible: it takes a fortnight to learn them. Pipes of affliction convey lukewarm water of affliction to some of the rooms, others more fortunate have fires. The garden is all heights, terraces, Excelsiors, misty mountain tops, seats up trees called Crows' Nests, flights of steps seemingly up to heaven lined with burning aspiration upon aspiration of scarlet geraniums: it is very pretty and airy but it gives you the impression that if you took a step farther you would find yourself somewhere on Plenlimmon, Conway Castle, or Salisbury Craig. With best love to detachments stationed at Hampstead believe me your loving son.

A Fine Prospect
Daniel Defoe

That which was most surprising, after such a tiresome and fatiguing journey, over the unhospitable mountains of Merioneth, and Carnarvonshire, was, that descending now from the hills, we came into a most pleasant, fruitful, populous, and delicious vale, full of villages and towns, the fields shining with corn, just ready for the reapers, the meadows green and flowery, and a fine river, with a mild and gentle; stream running through it: nor is it a small or casual intermission, but we had a prospect of the country open before us, for above 20 miles in length, and from 5 to 7 miles in breadth, all smiling with the same kind of complexion; which made us think ourselves in England again, all of a sudden.

from *A Tour Through the Whole Island of Great Britain* (1724)

A Walk Through Darkness
Glenda Beagan

The first time it was winter. February. Not cold though, really. She waited till six o'clock. Then all the people would be safe in their tall thin houses. She was afraid of her own transparency. That people could see. Light bulged from cracks in curtains, making bright oblongs on parked cars, on strips of privet. She slipped out quietly. Her mother was watching the News. In her mind's eye she saw deft fingers move over growing knitting, glasses perched low on her nose, lips softly counting.

She saw no one. It was easy. A dog barked somewhere. A cat appeared on a low wall, waiting to be fussed over, stroked, made much of. She gripped the torch in her pocket. She would not need it. An orange glow hummed over the town. As she left the flat streets and edged for the lanes, the farms, darkness did not make the sudden black shape she expected. The sky was a wedge of dark blue with still a pulse of light in it.

Her steps were quick and urgent. Strong. Telegraph poles whizzed by. Seemed to. Astonishing, this speed, this freedom. At the farm they were milking. Bold lights in the yard, the shippen doors held back, the rhythmic machines filling the night, making a focus of huddled roofs and walls. Caravans in the orchard under the great bare shape of the pear tree. Everything pared down to essentials. What did she feel? Exhilaration. Certainty.

Proper country now. A chill in the wind, a hint from the river. Her hands flex in her pockets. She brings out the torch. With deep glee she spins its light into the trees, the sycamore, its broad girth, the symmetry of its branches made spectral, gilded. She finds a child's abandon here, a kind of laughter, a bubble of it, anarchic, fierce, tinged with the joy of extremity. But she is not a child.

Over the first field. The cattle grid. She crosses it, rattling the metal bars. The track climbs steadily. Up there, high on the left, Top Farm in its fringe of poplars, its high gables peeping through twiggy swathes. Something that is neither moon nor starlight bathes the face of the house. No one lives there now, though sometimes, in daytime, it is still alive to the sound of tractors and trailers, collies yelping, boys swinging on gates. The house turns its emptiness, its serenity to the river, the whispering trees.

Over the first stile. It's muddy where she lands. Sheep move, soft grey shapes, too sleepy to bleat or warn. She has always had this ability, to move unannounced, unacknowledged among animals, as if accepted, as if part of their life, moving at a different pace, their pace, not part of the hectic life of humans. She walks with glad strides. Extravagant. The grass is longer, wetter. The sky is larger, a basin of deep sliding blue. The murmur of the river fills the air. Over the second stile. Into the lane. More mud. Stickier, then the central section, higher, firm with pebbles.

For centuries this track has led down to the ford, the only place to cross the river before the bridge was built. The first bridge. When was that? Twelfth century? She feels she is part of a pageant. An eighth century saint. A fourteenth century pilgrim. A friar, a Dominican, hooded in black. Soldiers and statesmen. Footpads. Rogues. The folk of the land. The folk blurring and blending. It's as if she hears the thumping of horses' hooves, the slow lumbering of wains, beasts driven to market. Flocks of geese. A dancing bear. Droves of children. She is glad to be saying goodbye.

There were picnics here with her own children. Years back. One more gate, a grey looming stone, the gate post, then the sloped field dips to the right, to a thicket of hazels and thorns. There, where the river makes its broad slow curve, silvery alders grow.

February Fill Dyke. That's what they say but the ground is surprisingly dry. Merely the hint of pulling earth on her shoes. There are cattle in the next field. They low softly. Her presence disturbs nothing. A waterbird, a coot, a moorhen, she can't see, moves unconcerned from the bank with only the faintest clatter. Movements, a chevron shape, on the dark water.

Everything is slowed, is stilled. Her own rage, if that's what it was, her own despair, if that's what it was, where are they now? She has walked for miles. She feels brightly alive. Tingling. Her skin is tingling. Warm with exertion while a cooling wind skims the river's smoothness. She sits on the bank, hugs her knees. Looks up at the sky's basin. Wonders why she came. Then the rain starts softly, hardly bothering to try.

from 'Seasonal Change' (1992)

Gwytherin
Ellis Peters

They turned aside from the Conway valley at Llanrwst, climbing away from the river into forested hill country. Beyond the watershed they crossed the Elwy where it is young and small, and moved steadily south-eastwards through thick woods, over another ridge of high land, to descend once again into the upland valley of a little river, that provided some marshy water meadows along its banks, and a narrow band of tilled fields, sloping and sturdy but protected by the forests, above these high pastures. The wooded ridge on either hand ran in oblique folds, richly green, hiding the scattered house-steads. The fields were already planted, and here and there orchards flowered. Below them, where the woods drew back to leave an amphitheatre of green, there was a small stone church, whitewashed and shimmering, and a little wooden house beside it.

'You see the goal of your pilgrimage,' said the chaplain Urien. He was a compact, neat, well-shaven personage, handsomely dressed and mounted, more of an ambassador than a clerk.

'That is Gwytherin?' asked Prior Robert.

'It is the church and priest's house of Gwytherin. The parish stretches for several miles along the river valley, and a mile or more from the Cledwen on either bank. We do not congregate in villages as you English do. Land good for hunting is plentiful, but good for tillage meagre. Every man lives where best suits him for working his fields and conserving his game.'

'It is a very fair place,' said the sub-prior, and meant it, for the fold on fold of well-treed hills beyond the river made a pattern of spring beauty in a hundred different greens, and the water-meadows were strung like a necklace of emeralds along the fringes of a necklace of silver and lapis-lazuli.

'Good to look at, hard to work,' said Urien practically, see there's an ox-team on the far side trying to break a new strip, now all the rest are planted. Watch the beasts strain at it, and you'll know how the higher ground weighs.'

Across the river, some way below them and a great way off, the snaky curve of the furrows already won patterned the slope between cultivated fields and leaning trees, a dark brown writing upon the hillside, and on the higher furrow, as yet uncompleted, the oxen leaned into their yokes and heaved, and the ploughman behind them clung and dragged at the heavy share. Before the leading pair a man walked backwards, arms gently waving and beckoning, his goad only a wand, flourished for magic, not for its sting, his high, pure calls carried aloft on the air, cajoling and praising. Towards him the beasts leaned willingly, following his cries with all their might. The new-turned soil, greyish-brown and sluggish, heaved moist and fresh to light after the share.

'A harsh country,' said Urien, as one assessing, not complaining, and set his horse moving downhill towards the church. 'Come, I'll hand you over to Father Huw, and see you well received.'

from *A Morbid Taste for Bones* (1977)

A View of the Clwyd
Joseph Hucks

. . . Our road became less interesting; and for ten or twelve miles, presented nothing to recompence the fatigue of a long and tedious walk, until we had ascended a very high hill, when the vale of Clwyd, in all its beauty, unfolded upon the sight: it appeared like a moving picture, upon which nature had been prodigal of its colours. Hamlets, villages, towns, and castles, rose like enchantment upon this rich carpet, that seemed covered with wood and enclosures; in the midst of it, at the distance of about five miles, the town of Ruthin, partially appeared from the bosom of a most beautiful grove of trees; the vale on each side being bounded by a chain of lofty mountains, and far off, on a bold and rugged promontory, stood Denbigh, with its strong fortress, the undisputed mistress of this extended scene. The great defect of the vale, is its want of water; the little river Clwyd, which winds through it, not being perceptible at any distance, and in dry seasons quite choaked up; though on the contrary, in wet and rainy weather, it soon overflows the whole country, swelled by the torrents from the surrounding hills.

from *A Pedestrian Tour Through North Wales in a Series of Letters*
edited by William Tydeman and Alun Jones (1799)

Dyserth Waterfall
Samuel Johnson

Stapylton's house is pretty: there are pleasing shades about it, with a constant spring that supplies a cold-bath. We then went to see a cascade.

I trudged unwillingly, and was not sorry to find it dry. The water was, however, turned on and produced a very striking cataract. They are paid an hundred pounds a year to divert the stream to the mines. The river, for such it may be termed, rises from a single spring, which, like that of Winifrede's, is covered with a building.

from *Diary of a Journey into North Wales* (1774)

At Variance
Anon.

Henllan church and Henllan steeple
Are the emblem of Henllan people,
All at variance,
What's the wonder,
When church and steeple are assunder.

An Instress and Charm
Gerard Manley Hopkins

Sept. 6. With Wm. Kerr, who took me up a hill behind ours (ours is Mynefyr), furze-grown and healthy hill, from which I could look round the whole country, up the valley towards Ruthin and down to the sea. The cleave in which Bodfari and Caerwys lie was close below. It was a leaden sky, braided or roped with cloud, and the earth in dead colours, grave but distinct. The heights by Snowdon were hidden by the clouds but not from distance or dimness. The nearer hills, the other side of the valley, shewed a hard and beautifully detached and glimmering brim against the light, which was lifting there. All the length of the valley the skyline of hills was flowingly written all along upon the sky. A blue bloom, a sort of meal, seemed to have spread upon the distant south, enclosed by a basin of hills. Looking all round but most in looking far up the valley I felt an instress and the charm of Wales.

from *Journals* (1874)

Hurrahing in Harvest
Gerard Manley Hopkins

Summer ends now; now, barbarous in beauty, the stooks rise
Around; up above, what wind-walks! what lovely behaviour
Of silk-sack clouds! has wilder, wilful-wavier
Meal-drift moulded ever and melted across skies?

I walk, I lift up, I lift up heart, eyes,
Down all that glory in the heavens to glean our Saviour;
And éyes, heárt, what looks, what lips yet gave you a
Rapturous love's greeting of realer, of rounder replies?

And the azurous hung hills are his world-wielding shoulder
Majestic — as a stallion stalwart, very-violet-sweet! —
These things, these things were here and but the beholder
Wanting; which two when they once meet,
The heart rears wings bold and bolder
And hurls for him, O half hurls earth for him off under his feet.

Elwy and Clwyd
W.T. Palmer

Elwy and Clwyd are twin rivers of the gentlest vale in all Wales, a vale which slopes 30 miles to the sea, with poplar-lined roads, with towered and spired churches and hamlets creeping beneath rich woods. Elwy comes down the west side; Clwyd drains the east, and because it traps more streams from the moorland glens, it becomes the main stream at Rhuddlan, where the two come together. Yet they are different in character: in a hundred yards one can pick out the stream. Here we stand by a ford on Elwy — a bright ripple runs over the stones; there is a golden cloud of tansy and ragwort among the pebbles, of devil's rhubarb and coltsfoot on the banks, of willow-herb and forget-me-not rooted in the mud. And on the sods here and there are balsam or touch-me-not, with monkey-plant or wild musk-plants which are alleged to be aliens in this district, yet cannot have come there from any garden.

Clwyd is different; its pools are always misty, with suspended limestone dust which settles down into a soft mud, so that one can only cross from bank to bank at the points where a bar of pebbles or ledge of rock shows its vicinity by broken water. The banks are apt to be hollowed and unsafe, and the streams have deep pools. Step a foot from the sound bar, and you have a glorious splash in a yard of water. It is well to watch where the cattle cross — but in many cases a wire fence keeps the stock to one side or the other, or cuts it away altogether except at recognized drinking places, where the shore is trodden into deep sludge. And Clwyd meanders in and out without any great determination to push on to the sea. Indeed, the water level at St. Asaph is not much higher than at Rhuddlan, where legend says that English warships floated from the sea up to wharves outside the old castle gate.

Elwy has character; its music is sprightly, and one is not disappointed in the fighting powers of its trout. Granted they do not run as large as those from the other stream, they are still satisfactory, and in colour they are more brilliant. However, that is a topic on which local anglers can never agree. The lures on Elwy are always heavier than the light 'drys' customary on the Clwyd. Clwyd, moreover, does not fish well in calm weather; it needs a strong wind to ruffle its pools; but Elwy, though less fine in its supreme moments, is more consistent. One can always pick up a few fish if the weather be anything but sky-clear.

Clwyd has the more history; it comes down past Ruthin and Denbigh castles; but Elwy has only a moorland story. The Llansannan gorge is fine — perhaps that is why the prattle of Elwy is always merry. It has never the deep pools of mystery which Clwyd brings down from the fighting frontier of old Wales. But Elwy was more a fastness of the old nation; its gorges held their armies, and hid their farms from the Saxons until time to sally out, replenished as to stores and refreshed as to spirit, to make another stroke against the invaders. The great moor of Elwy has its own secrets, but they are not voiced by its rivulets.

I like to think of Clwyd as a stream in which cattle stand to drink; it is soft, peaceful, reflecting their colours and shapes on its smooth surface; but Elwy, by the same token, should be the stream of the mountain ponies which scamper about the pastures beneath the heather moors. Elwy has not the rushing quality of the Conway streams and those round Snowdon, which are linked with the wild mountain sheep. Both streams pour through wooded defiles, but

Clwyd long ago threw off the narrow wilderness, and has floated for leagues beneath poplars and great willows, among park land studded with oaks and chestnuts, rather than among the stunted alders, whose roots hang down the rocks. Here again is contrast to anyone who cares to walk a mile alongside the banks of each stream.

from *More Odd Corners in North Wales* (1944)

Shaman

Glenda Beagan

To find a speech, a tongue
to fit interstices
of this land worn close as a skin.

To climb among blackthorn, cold
cupping of bud white
on black twigs; a scent

is there, thin and shining
as cowslips in floodweather, under
skies of dark geese, deep eddies

of cloud. Here, the high bank
crumbles; fragile roots are prinked
with gobbets of red earth.

What is the sound this land makes
at the far reach of March,
with the lengthening sun, a cleanness

of fresh sap? The speech
of the shaman is locked in the water web
where rivers meet; slowdeep

valley wanderer of the wide meander,
still chuckling mountain freshet,
spate river, riding on pebbles,

not mud, blending watery selves,
distinct as people, below Rhydyddauddwr.
Incompatible, are they; slow sluggish

dark flow, quick moody swift
young sprinter to the sea? It was
like this a millennium earlier,

at the crossing place. Hear heavy wains,
the whinny of horses, the voices in the dusk —
chill calls, that Norman French nasality,

Tegeingl mingling Mercian; vowels, broadening,
lengthening, but never merging with the plaited water
nor interweaving on a loom of moisture.

The threads remain; sharp, several, sure.

(This poem was prompted by some reflections on the meeting of the rivers Elwy and Clwyd.)

In the Valley of the Elwy
Gerard Manley Hopkins

I remember a house where all were good
To me, God knows, deserving no such thing:
Comforting smell breathed at very entering,
Fetched fresh, as I suppose, off some sweet wood.
That cordial air made those kind people a hood
All over, as a bevy of eggs the mothering wing
Will, or mild nights the new morsels of Spring:
Why, it seemed of course; seemed of right it should.

Lovely the woods, waters, meadows, combes, vales,
All the air things wear that build this world of Wales;
Only the inmate does not correspond:
God, lover of souls, swaying considerate scales
Complete thy creature dear O where it fails,
Being mighty a master, being a father and fond.

The House on the Moors

Lord Devonport

In the early nineties of the last century my father built a shooting box in North Wales some 10 miles from Denbigh on the Pentre Foelas road. The house, a wooden one, stood at over 1,600 feet and was said to be the highest private house in Britain. It was built in Norway, taken to pieces, and re-erected in North Wales, three Norwegians coming over to help re-erect it. Where my father got the idea of buying a Norwegian wooden house I have no notion.

The house was called Gwylfa Hiraethog, which in Welsh means The Watch Tower of the Hiraethog mountains. It was aptly named; it was said to be screwed to the rock.

The view from the house was unique and it was generally considered to have the finest view in the British Isles. On a fine day, one could see the whole of the Snowdon range, and the Irish Sea to the north-west.

During the 28 years we owned it and lived in it as a shooting box in the autumn, on three occasions only we were able to see the Isle of Man, the Mourne mountains in Ulster and once only the Mull of Galloway in Wigtownshire about 100 miles away.

My father's business partner had a house in Ulster in the Mourne mountains. My father sent him a replied paid telegram (we had no telephone in those days) saying 'We can see you. Can you see us?' to which my father's partner replied 'Yes, ditto.'

The phenomenon only occurred in exceptional circumstances when we got incredible visibility always followed by a terrific south-west gale.

The annual visit to Gwylfa Hiraethog caused great excitement to my sister, my brother and myself. The journey from London was made by train. At Chester, our special coach was detached from the London train and shunted on to the Denbigh train, which made fourteen stops before reaching its destination. As the train neared Bodfari we looked eagerly out of the train window. If it was fine we could see Gwylfa Hiraethog crowning the hilltop some 15 miles away.

At Denbigh station a pair horse wagonette met us, but before leaving the town we would stop at the Crown Hotel, to have egg and rhubarb jam with our tea. Rhubarb seemed very popular in Wales in those days.

The Crown was kept by a Mrs Hughes, an ardent Liberal. My father was also a Liberal and always chose the Crown for that reason. Another hotel, the Bull was the better of the two, but it was a Conservative hotel.

After tea, we began our long uphill drive to Gwylfa. There was a steady rise of 1,557 feet. There was something exhilarating in the air living at over 1,600 feet. All around for miles was nothing but heather. There was no garden at Gwylfa; the heather came right up to the house and many a time as a child, looking out of my nursery window in the early morning, I saw grouse standing on the front door steps.

Every day during the shooting season, a dogcart was sent to Denbigh to fetch the mail, papers and provisions.

At Gwylfa, we burnt nothing but peat except in the kitchen range. For this, coal was required and this also had to be hauled up some 1,500 feet from Denbigh. The journey took three hours.

Gwylfa, standing at that height, was exposed to winds of a gale force. I remembered an elderly lady setting out for a walk one windy day. She had only got a short distance when a gust of wind lifted her off her feet, her voluminous skirts and petticoats as worn by women in those days, acting as a balloon.

In 1925 my father decided to sell. Gwylfa was never again inhabited. There was a suggestion of converting the house into an hotel but at such a height no one would look at it. In spite of its wonderful position and views, one could not expect tourists for more than five months in the year. For weeks the house might be enveloped in mist and in winter it could be snowed up for long periods. Keeping domestic staff ten miles from the town, without amusements for guests or staff, just did not make sense.

Exposed for over 40 years to all the winds that blow, Gwylfa is now gradually falling to pieces. Windows and doors have long since disappeared and the last time I saw it, in 1966, sheep, sheltering against the gale, were lying huddled in the drawing room.

an article in *Country Quest* (1968)

Gwylfa Hiraethog
Wilson MacArthur

In the distance stood a great gaunt building by itself, in a vast fenced enclosure where something of an attempt at gardening still remained, and we went through the gate and up the drive to inspect, at close quarters, one of those occasional monuments of the days when a section of society still existed with the means to indulge a whim or folly in the grand manner.

It was a shooting-box with the dimensions of a great mansion and it was falling rapidly into decay and ruin. It commanded views of superb magnificence out over the great moors, and in its absolute isolation what brief elegance had it sported, what short-lived triumph of ingenuity over desolation, as if one were to erect and maintain some super Savoy Hotel in Tamanrasset or In Guezzam in the Sahara Desert or a Sandringham at Putnam's Camp in the Congo. Brief and short-lived; for it was not old, hardly older than the century, if that, and the disproportion of its usefulness to its cost must stand as one of the last follies of a social system now disrupted. Yet one could not but feel some latent sympathy with the man who had built it, seeking, it seemed, some philosophic pinnacle of detachment from which to survey a bewildering world. Time and the weather were taking their rapid toll and we looked in upon once gracious rooms now derelict and in eclipse, with peeling plaster and stained ceilings and splendour all decayed; then, as the high moorland wind was cold, and colder with each moment that brought the night nearer, we returned to the road and the long line of cars and waited only briefly before we set off to regain the companionship of the River Conway.

from *The River Conway* (1952)

A Trip to Llety'r Eos

Alun Llywelyn-Williams

Surely the nightingale will not sing in this snowy night:
it is a mystery how the grey singer ever ventured,
some incredible summers ago, so far from the lowland
trees, so close to the pallid heavens of Hiraethog.

Eight hundred feet up, the snow begins to stick, the night
becomes bright; along the white hedges the car's wide
headlamps skate smoothly, but the wheels squeak 'careful!'
We slow down, and turn cautiously at the high crossroad.

Topography

We gape from our small guided world at the purity
of the calm sheepwalks' cosmos; the shut gates
slip past one by one, and the grey lines
of cowshed and cottage pour sleep to their centre.

Dark, chirpless, the sentinel grove on the brow of the hill;
but through the last welcoming gate, the lawn gleams,
a spotless glade, and the house beyond takes shape
from the white conquest like an enduring continent.

When the auto stands at the gate, when the door is opened,
the snow's smothering muteness is flung back to the night
by the voices of welcome, and the cheerful chat of the fire
and the light of fellowship on the hearth of the summerhouse of song.

trans. Joseph P. Clancy

Cerrigydruddian

Peter Marshall

Drizzle immemorial
dragged me back
to scratch the prodigal itch.
Chingachgook remains,
older now, passive,
chromium mount
tethered to pitting asphalt.

The rasher's smile
still bleeds ketchup,
while Cook thumbs ants
on curling formica;
Elvis lives
in the tardis,
but croons a different tune.

Birchbark savages ooze
yellow as yolk
onto my plate,
and I can almost hear

the crackle of pine musketry,
smell his old holborne cardy,
visualize her madness
dancing with the dust;

but the images sting,
like slapped legs.

Outside foxgloves wave:
love letters in the sand
warp by the pigbin's peel;
the urinals reek
and seem to bubble burdock;
sacrificial longlegs
dangle hideously
from greying webs.

Our heraldic runes,
carved so many years before,
remain in slate;
porcelain towns,
no mystery now,
brown sadly in china.

Opal fruits
and ice cream:
I leave the place haunted,
glancing back,
like an infant
fleeing from the dark.

Coastal Erosion

Sue Trevelyan-Jones

At the beginning of this century, evidence was being collected in connection with a property dispute. When asked to indicate the whereabouts of the cottage where she was born, an old woman, to everyone's astonishment, pointed out to sea. However, the foundations of a cottage were found below high water mark and for some years a mound of sand marked the spot until it was smoothed out by the tide.

Further evidence that the coastline used to be a considerable distance out to sea comes from the Reverend Robert Williams in his 'History of Aberconwy' 1835 and from Mr. William Ashton who writes, 'The ancient lost land north of Colwyn was protected by Muriau or walls, signs of which may still be seen on a very low ebb of the tide in the shape of a long line of surf as the waves break upon them. The walls are said to run about a mile from shore for about four miles in a west to east direction.' The sea is generally fairly shallow and between Rhos and Old Colwyn there is an extensive sandbank lying a couple of miles offshore. This is the Constable Bank; a narrow shandy shoal running for about ten miles east of the Great Orme.

Inundations by the sea have occurred throughout history all along the coast from the River Dee to the Menai Straits. In fact, any coastline is only a transitory feature being subject to deposition or erosion by the force of the sea, and to long slow earth movements producing a gradual uplift or subsidence of an area.

For centuries our coastline locally has been subject to a combination of erosion and apparent subsidence which has gradually pushed it further inland. It is believed to have originally extended out almost to the Point of Ayr and records of the sea's gradual encroachment can be found going back to the sixth century. In the churchyard of St. Michael's, Abergele, there is an undated tombstone set into the wall bearing an inscription indicating that the deceased had lived three miles to the north. As Abergele is now only one mile from the sea, the deceased's home now lies on the seabed two miles out from shore. Pennant in his 'Journeyings in North Wales', published in 1778, mentions that he had seen at low tide, a long stretch of land well away from shore full of the trunks of oak trees, whole, but so soft they could be cut with a knife. Tree roots have also been seen at low tide in the sand at Rhos-on-Sea.

from *When the Sea Came By*, edited by Malcolm Jones (1992)

A Victorian Hotel

George Porter

Pwllycrochan was opened as a hotel one day in June 1866; some visitors drove over from Llandudno to lunch, and on that day, in the opinion of most people, Colwyn Bay as a resort, was born.

With the aid of the map and the recollections of childhood I must try to describe the now almost unbelievably rustic surroundings of the place in 1866. If in those days a visitor emerged from the hotel on a walk to the station he would at once find himself on a private drive fenced off by light wire railings from spacious parks on either side. Looking over his right shoulder towards the woods, he would see the arbutus tree, now in the middle of a road, growing in the East Park. After passing through a gate he would see through a screen of trees Pwllycrochan Isaf farm and from there on, the farm road and the drive, separated by a hedge, ran side by side to the turnpike road. After passing through the final gate (marked in the map), he would find himself on the main road about fifty yards west of the present junction. He would then walk between hedges on a purely country road to the tollbar and down the lane to the diminutive Colwyn station, then partially encircled by a dingle. During the whole of his walk, with the exception of the tollbar, he would not have passed a single building, and quite probably have not met a single soul. As likely as not he would have heard a covey of partridges whirring over his head.

It was some years before the features the mansion had possessed as a squire's residence were modified or abolished. The shooting was kept up and game abundant, the gamekeeper living in Rhiw Bach.

Small bird-life is still plentiful, but in those days the rasp of the corncrake could be heard in the fields, and sparrow- and kestrel-hawks nested in the woods, while herons and kingfishers haunted the weir.

Squirrels were numerous, especially along the old road in autumn among the chestnuts. Hounds occasionally met in front of the hotel. We children (there were six of us) found a magnificent play ground for mischief and adventure in the large rambling outhouses, gardens, fields, and natural sea shore — not to mention the (to us) illimitable forest at the back, with its mysterious pools, dark dells and other objects of curiosity mixed with fear. Donkeys were our favourite means of transport. On donkeys we made the great journey to Coed Coch to fetch toy bricks from the sawmill there; on donkeys we took telegrams to our nearest telegraph office, Old Colwyn, and on donkeys we rode over the hill to our tailor in Mochdre, Mr. Daniel Davies. We liked this ride, as, after measuring his young clients, old Daniel would present them with gingerbreads and other delicacies produced from the miniature Selfridge's store which he kept. For orchestral music we relied on wandering German brass-bands, whose music reminded us of the braying of our donkeys; but we had something much better on Saturday nights, when the Colwyn band came along and performed in front of the hotel. Yet to come were high-brow entertainments in a mission room which once stood in St. Paul's grounds. These consisted of amateur concerts and penny readings, with the vicar of Llandrillo in the chair.

In the house itself were some interesting features Before the range in the kitchen hung an old-fashioned spit geared up above to a shaft which led to a wheel in a small recess where the turnspit could turn an ordinary wheel-handle and so keep the joint revolving in front of the fire. In the still-room was a most handsome wooden mantelpiece carved in high relief to represent the fable of the fox and the stork. Outside, the outhouses seemed endless; all buildings necessary for carriages and about twelve horses; dog-kennels, a large laundry, a brewery, a fruit-room, and many other storehouses. Perhaps the prettiest feature of the place was a drying-green — a glade in the wood planted with orderly rows of small hedges on which washing was spread out to dry and in which many birds built their nests.

from *Colwyn Bay Before the Houses Came* (1938)

This Stretch of Lovely Coast
H.V. Morton

Along the forty-odd miles of this road between Rhyl and Caernarvon are dotted some of the best-known and best-liked towns in the whole of Wales. This stretch of lovely coast is the playground of the industrial cities of the Midlands and the North. No true Midlander and no true son of Lancashire is entirely ignorant of it. It is a part of Wales designed by Nature and Man to capture the leisure moments of crowds.

Rhyl, Colwyn Bay and Llandudno are, of course, the big favourites on this coast-line, but between them are quiet little places, such as Pensarn, with Abergele and its woody hills at the back, and Llandulas where poor Richard II was betrayed into the hands of Bolingbroke.

It is not difficult to see why Colwyn Bay has become one of the most popular places in North Wales. Gold sands, a great half circle of sea, hills, woods and streams. The semi-circle of hills on the south and west give to this place what doctors call a 'local climate'. Like all these northern watering-places in Wales a large part of their charm and popularity is due to the fact that you can be tucked away in the town, but half an hour's walking takes you to hills and winds from the Atlantic.

from *In Search of Wales* (1933)

Rhyl Sands
Adrian Henri

Your vision swept clear and bright by the wind that's wiping away the stormclouds
beach low and empty pale blue sky, seagulls and one dog near the horizon
pebbles underfoot as clear as the wallpaper in seaside cafes
somewhere out at sea, a rainbow
the sad peeling offseason colours of arcades and kiosks
David Cox's 'Rhyl Sands' a tiny gem burning quietly in dirty Manchester
ghostly echoes of last season's chip-papers in the drifting sand...

water foaming and fizzing round your warm body
sudden rush upwards green light everywhere
sharp salty taste in your mouth your nose stinging
down again gasping your breath in
sounds rushing in cries of bathers distant children
the promenade the Pavilion bright like a postcard

from *Autobiography* (1980)

Venice in Wales
Harry Thomas

Built in 1892, and opened in 1902, it was described as 'surpassing anything previously attempted in North Wales and anything previously known in the history of Rhyl.'

The Queens Palace was a luxurious building of four storeys which accommodated a large theatre and ballroom reputed at the time to be the largest in Britain — if not the world.

There was also a huge shopping complex, complete with a fountain and fernery. The wooden floor to the market was the original ballroom, open from 10.30 am until 10.30 pm.

Admission to the whole Queens Palace complex was 1/6d (8p). Underneath the Palace's huge dome were exotic tropical plants and a zoo, complete with various side-shows and a popular monkey house, and an Ashanti village complete with 'natives' living in grass huts.

There was a 'modern-day' passenger lift near to the entrance of the 'Venice' attraction which visitors could take to the small viewing tower above the dome, and on a clear day you would be able to see the Isle of Man, Snowdon and the hills of Ireland.

Beneath the Queens Palace ground level was the 'Venice' which attracted large crowds. Admission to view this unique attraction was 2d (1p), while a trip on the gondolas was an extra 1d.

The 'Venice' was a representation of the water city of Venice, only on a miniature scale. A description at the time read: 'Not only are the walls of the buildings adorned at great expense with faithful likeness of present-day Venetian scenes, but even the eight double arches that span the walled-in water, on which real gondolas are propelled by real Italians are treated in a style that should satisfy the most fastidious tastes.

'Gondolas take visitors around the canals and in and out of the arches in truly Venetian fashions. Even the ceiling is star-spangled so that at night, when the 100 electric lamps are aglow, it is delightful to contemplate.'

Sadly, in 1907, only five years after its opening, the unique Victorian structure that was the Queens Palace was totally destroyed by fire.

If the Queens had survived, it would possibly have been the world's greatest attraction, here in Wales.

from *The Rhyl Journal*, 27 October 1993

Today

Bryan Aspden

We visit Prestatyn. From limestone hill
look down, like kestrels, on the holiday
seaside town. This is called Fish Mountain,
high land where once the ocean had its way.
Here one inch deep is fathoms of grey bone,
a hardened sea where skeleton and shell
swim in the undercurrents of the hill
and fish have surfaced from the stone.
Quarry scree fans to an estuary.
We settle beside it, start our picnic.
Curled like a question mark a cat suggests
another world of time where hardness
melts and flows, no barrier's placed between
stone and sea, stillness and motion.

On this quarry floor, hacked from the ocean,
Buddleia, Old Man's Beard, blue butterflies
scent and stain, inscribe the air, bright living
offsets of a fossiled shore. These are death's
afterthoughts the cat from its bramble
tunnel understands, for it has tested
with micro-sensitive paws both worlds
that merge, are one, and then are parted.
Here too is where division's signposted:
'Llwybr Clawdd Offa. Offa's Dyke Path';
with a concrete acorn underneath.
Stone in a waterdrop suspended falls.
I watch and wonder what language will be
spoken here when the stone has turned to sea.

from *News of the Changes* (1984)

The Sands of Dee
Charles Kingsley

'O Mary, go and call the cattle home,
And call the cattle home,
And call the cattle home
Across the sands of Dee.'
The western wind was wild and dark with foam,
And all alone went she.

The western tide crept up along the sand,
And o'er and o'er the hand,
And round and round the sand,
As far as eye could see.
The rolling mist came down and hid the land;
And never home came she.

'O is it weed or fish or floating hair —
A tress of golden hair,
A drowned maiden's hair,
Above the nets at sea?'
Was never salmon yet that shone so fair
Among the stakes of Dee.

They rowed her in across the rolling foam,
The cruel crawling foam,
The cruel hungry foam,
To her grave beside the sea,
But still the boatmen hear her call the cattle home,
Across the sands of Dee.

Alton Locke (1850)

Wildfowling on the Welsh Side
Leslie Brockbank

Our visits to the Welsh side were based entirely on the habits of the duck. Our purpose in going out well before daylight was not always to shoot but to study the birds. We have left the birds many, many times when we could have taken a good shot but we just were not satisfied. For instance I think we had every wigeon in the river in a gutter at Llanerchymor on one occasion. Just at the crucial moment a fellow came out from Rhyl or Bodfari, flew his plane just over our heads and put the birds out. We were so thrilled with this tremendous pack of wigeon that we decided we would go back every day to see if they mustered there again. We went down a number of times and a fortnight later they were there again in exactly the same spot, just where we wanted them. And I'm hanged if the fellow didn't come out again and spoil it for us! We used to get up that end well before daylight and then work right down to Mostyn either through the Welshman's Gutter or through the Shrouds.

We used to stay sometimes at the Ship Inn, Connahs Quay, and could come down to meet Leonard Brooke on the river. He stayed at the Quay House and we were always careful to be out before him in the mornings! On one occasion I was told that his house-keeper had phoned him at his Liverpool office to say, 'There is a man on the river shooting your ducks'.

Once we were coming up the buoys from Mostyn and we saw mallard 'standing on each others heads', to quote Monk, at Bagillt. The trammelling boats were coming up on the flood behind us and there was just no way into the birds even though the fishermen held back for us. We hung back for as long as we could and then went in, but just as we were getting close one of the fishermen called across to another boat and all the birds went up with a roar of wings.

On another occasion just at dusk with a yellow glow in the sky we heard from the fishermen, who were holding back to give us a chance, that there were any number of duck in Bagillt. It was rather a nice gesture and although we had no shot we must have seen between three and four hundred mallard.

from *Dee Wildfowler* (1982)

The All-Knowing Dee

Michael Drayton

. . . Twice under earth her crystal head doth run:
When instantly again Dee's holiness begun,
By his contracted front and sterner waves, to shew

That he had things to speak might profit us to know;
A brook that was suppos'd much business to have seen
Which had an ancient bound 'twixt Wales and England been,
And noted was by both to be an ominous flood,
That, changing of his fords, the future ill or good
Of either country told, of either's war or peace,
The sickness or the health, the dearth or the increase;
And that of all the floods of Britain, he might boast
His stream in former times to have been honour'd most.

from *Polyalbion* (1622)

The Divinity of the Dee
John Rhys

'Every locality had its divinity, and the rivers were especially identified with certain divine beings, as witness the streams that still bear the name of Dee and kindred ones. The Dee or *Deva* of North Wales had another name, which appears in Welsh literature as Aerven or the genius of war; and so late as the time of Giraldus it retained some of its ancient prestige: it was still supposed to indicate beforehand the event of the frequent wars between the Welsh and the English by eating away its banks on the Welsh or the English side, as the case might be.

from *Celtic Britain* (1882)

Wet Spring Bank Holiday, Dee Estuary
Gladys Mary Coles

Most of the view you have to imagine
when grey presents its variations —
the opposite coast ghosting back.
Absent first are the field shapes?
a green collage of hills,
precise definition of copse and farm,

the massed browns of Holywell;
next, Moel-y-Parc retracts its long antenna.
Under a gauze of rain, the outlined hills —
curvilinear, cut-off, cauled —
disappear in the drowned distance.

From both the estuary's shores
this same shroud separating
coasts, cliffs, the sprinkling of estates
whose lights at night are fallen galaxies —
all dissolve in the vanishing trick.

The metallic Dee divides
yet magnetises shore to shore.
Staring across from each side, eyes
watch like wildlife in undergrowth;
or binocularised, strain to reduce the miles,
capture circles of someone else's space.
Dunlin, redshank, gull, in flight
link coast to coast invisibly,
alight on unseen sand-banks.

Always there's this yearning to connect —
the views are never sufficient,
yet every fade-out seems somehow a death.

from *The Glass Island* (1992)

An Estuary View
Emyr Humphreys

Seven o'clock in the morning. Standing on top of the old lime kiln, Richard Bloyd glanced at his wrist-watch, held it close to his ear, and then plunged his hands once more deep into his overcoat pockets. It was a fine morning, but still chilly. Across the water he saw the Wirral emerge from the early morning mist; become once more a solid and substantial rich-green sea-girt land, speckled with red-roofed houses. The tide was out and down the estuary the mud flats gleamed in the oblique rays of the sun like the backs of enormous slugs resting in the low water. Down below on the water's edge the colliery's gaunt cranes emerged from a pall of mist and smoke, in its small harbour a dirty steamer blew its fog-horn into the silence, and after the silence was broken the day awoke. A train raced urgently across the coastal plain, as though all consideration was over, all decisions made, and the execution of plans begun.

from *The Little Kingdom* (1946)

Shotton
John Richards

A rapid helter-skelter down King Edward Street in order to dash into the expansive waistcoat of my returning father as the battalions of clogged men trudged wearily from the river with their empty beer bottles slanting askew, almost falling out of their pockets. I can still smell that sweaty acidic smell of the Courtaulds ladies in shapeless, faded, water-pink overalls as they too plodded from the station — always, it seemed, at the darkening. Those emotive memories were real to me as they must have been to others. There is now only the indifference of old age.

If I had realised it, the future vista must have been coloured by those Shotton streets. Had I but known it, all those august cathedrals, including Lincoln and Chartres, were mere replicas of St Ethelwold's! The main road was as wide as any market square near St. Mark's square in Venice, a square which was never a square. How dare anyone say that the most beautiful road in Shotton was the main road which led out of it! The broad dignity of the 'Road' was enhanced by the 'England expects' signal bunting hoisted every Trafalgar Day near the church school cannon. Imagination, of course, but we were children and such scenes as these with the May Pole on the empty ground between Lodwicks and the school, made up for the parallel rows of begrimed brick houses with their muddy and cinder hardened backs. There seemed to be smoke everywhere, belching out of the chimneys high on the sharp angled black slate roofs like 'lids', standing in their environs of wilfully besmirched dreariness. Much of this atmosphere drifted on the winds from that 'momentus hive' across the river — even the sulphur could be tasted at the back of the throat, however, we had our rainbows. The silver cup by the Quay Team was exhibited proudly in Knowles' shop window and was viewed with an overwhelming pride. 'The Quay had won again!' were words of stimulating magic to the little lads of thereabouts.

from *Memories: Reminiscences of Deeside* (ed. Joan Owesu 1993)

New spaces, Clwyd

John Davies

Near here are places we've seeped away from.
Half-blind, Talacre lighthouse peers inland
over waves of marram grass and dunes
unrolling, a white stick in its hand.
Sun tilts. A farmhouse opposite ships light
going down nameless on the hill
to mark, with the lighthouse, claims
wreckage makes to our emptied spaces still.

We have trees between us, wild nights they pace
the gardens. Leaves are where they've been.
Wires sing and sing. Skittering past
are roads burnished to a sheen
by the lamps our homes grip tightly.
Water, sighing, turns and tosses under cover,
our shadow life that does not dream of us.
Only pavements hear it stir.

And now there are places in town
that have lately seeped from us. Around
the railway station, small factories
unloading shadow on patches of waste ground
await deliverance from empty car parks.
There are shops white-windowed with surprise.
Unfinished buildings, gestures frozen
by bad news, from tumbled sites half-rise.

But, too, space some fill with themselves.
Clouds break like surf on the sun,
it won't go out. It shines through you
around me who, alive, see what's begun
anew when rain in lit streets glints tinfoil
or a pane's stained glassiness shows trees
more real than trees. You remind me that in space
are dim scatters bursting as discoveries.

from *The Visitor's Book* (1985)

Rhosllanerchrugog

Raymond Edwards

Most Welsh people have grown up in a small town or big town, small village or big village. Mine was a big village —the biggest, if you believe the statisticians, not only in Wales but in the whole of the United Kingdom, some 15,000 of us somehow managed to live there, and not an architect or town planner among us. It was not the kind of village which attracts sight-seers, and if any came to Rhosllanerchrugog, it would be due to going off course on the main Ruabon Wrexham road.

Such an error would involve them in a steep, mile-long climb to this isolated encampment. The place itself was a maze of narrow streets without pavements, streets which seemed to have been pushed between the red terracotta brick houses. The air was full of smoke at all seasons, for the majority of the menfolk were miners, and coal was cheap to burn. They couldn't be prodigal with much else.

The colliery, ironically called Hafod ('a Summer dwelling') was conveniently situated a mile away, a golden mile of insulation between it and the villagers, a place where the men met to work and talk. In the middle of the sprawling rash of houses were schools, chapels, public houses, a football field, aptly named Cae-dwr ('water field') and a miners' institute comprising a cinema-cum-concert hall, a lesser hall, a billiards room, draughts and chess room, committee rooms, and a library.

This was my home town, grim and unprepossessing, a place most people would shun, apart from the 15,000 to whom it meant and means something special. You couldn't shake it off, it got into the marrow and it remains.

If there was something about the place, there was something about its people too. They were a trilingual people, Welsh, English and often a curious amalgam of both. The men, like most Welsh miners, were blessed with splendid voices. The job, I'm sure, helps the voice — working underground, breathing deeply, nostrils dilated, cavernous mouths, chests distended, waists belted, abdomens pressed, resonating chambers fully operational what comes naturally to the miner has to be taught as a method to the actor and singer.

They were a robust people, many with little formal education, but with alert inquiring minds, wide general knowledge, initiative and adaptability. They worked hard and played harder. They were village people with urban tastes. They enjoyed sport, and in particular, music and drama, the urban arts which only thrive where there is a large population to sustain them. These public arts, in turn, integrated the community, for there were two large choirs — a mixed and a male — an opera company, an orchestra and a drama company.

As part of this tribal community we learnt to survive in a crowd early in life. Most of the things we did, we did in groups, and there were few solitary pastimes. We learnt to think big, to assert, to push with cocksure arrogance in a highly competitive society. We were the champions. We even referred to the people of neighbouring villages as *pobl yr ochr draw*, the people on the other side of the hill — and not just geographically.

from *Artists in Wales* (ed. Meic Stephens, 1973)

A Winter Journey
Oliver Onions

Men cursed the icy wind that now blew straight at their backs, and now that they had got it going again the sow did not stop, and Willie, clambering out of its flap while it was still on the move, knew the signs of snow when he saw them. It began in fact to fall that very morning. Slowly treetop and hillside greyed, whitened, and the oxen were given no rest, for siege-towers on the road were trouble enough without snow. The white flakes settled on shoulders and crusted on the iron sallets, and now even their destination had to be changed. It was to have been Berwyn, hard by Valle Crucis. Now it was good-bye Berwyn, for they would be lucky if they made Wrexham that night.

Yet not even of Wrexham had Willie more than a glimpse. The coming of the snow had spurred other travellers to haste too, and coming out of the town with the snow still falling steadily and without a break, was a company that could not have far to go, for otherwise it would not have been so foolhardy as to set out. They were in fact going no further than Valle Crucis, now a bare dozen miles away, and what was a hindrance to them was a boon to Matthias, who now that he was rested again could keep up with their slowed-down pace with ease.

Valle Crucis stood by its stream, its great eastern face mitred with white, its five towering windows ledged and cornered with snow. Its vast courtyard, at other times as busy as a fair with merchants, hucksters; pilgrims, men-at-arms and those of every make and sort from the outside world, was a white and deserted square. The porter asked their business, not as refusing them but as ascertaining their station, and those in charge of horses were shown to the stables at the north of the forecourt, their masters to the row of buildings to the south of it. Before them rose the great west door of the church, with the cloister-porter's lodge in the shadow of it, and to all his dreaming Willie now finally said good-bye, for everything had settled itself over his head. He and Matthias were conducted to the pilgrim's lodging until the prior should have given further directions. So, stamping the snow from their feet, they reached their winter quarters.

from *Poor Man's Tapestry* (1946)

At Valle Crucis Abbey

A.G. Prys-Jones

For centuries the kindly grass
Has clothed the Abbey's scattered stones,
And tenderly the twining trees
Have bound the chancel's fractured bones;
Deep-rooted round this ruined house of prayer

The starry hawthorn and the wild, red rose
Perform their faithful ministries, aware
That every Spring along this hidden glen
The angel of the sanctuary comes and goes
Through aisles of blossom nurtured by the dust
Of prince and peasant, poet and chronicler
Devout or wayward who at last
Found benison and burial here.

And I, in this green, hallowed place,
Was drawn within the silence there,
A realm where language, time and space
Dissolved upon the crystal air;
And all the vale leapt bright with sudden change
To beauty more intense than flaring fire,
Shining with symbols rich and rare and strange,
Until in soaring music, sweet and long,
The birds about the broken choir
Poured forth their hymns of praise in ardent song.

Llangollen Ale

Anon.

While other poets loudly rant
About Llangollen's Vale,
Let me, with better taste, descant
Upon Llangollen Ale.

The daughters of the place are fair,
Its sons are strong and hale:
What makes them so? Llangollen air?
No, no! — Llangollen Ale.

And Nature only beautified
The landscape, to prevail
On travellers to turn aside
And quaff Llangollen Ale.

For though the scene might please at first
Its charms would quickly stale;
While he who tastes will ever thirst
To drink Llangollen Ale.

In short, each ruin, stream, or tree,
Within Llangollen's Tale,
Wherever I turn, whate'er I see,
Is redolent of Ale.

(Nineteenth Century)

A Wonder of the Age
Jan Morris

Up a farm road near Tremeirchion in Clwyd there stands a very strange structure indeed. It is evidently all that is left of a much larger building around an open court, and it is built of red brick on a palatial scale, and has classical pilasters attached to it, and is hugely embelished with the initials RC and the date 1567. It does not feel like Wales at all, but more like the yard of a Swedish castle, or something in Jutland. It was an early example of exoticism, not to say high jinks, in the houses of the Welsh gentry.

True, Sir Richard Clough's Plas Bach-y-Graig was an eccentric affair from the first. Clough himself was unusual enough — a draper's son from Denbigh who made an immense fortune in Antwerp, returned to Clwyd to be one of Katheryn of Berain's husbands, and died in his forty-first year — and his great house was much in his own style. It was the first Welsh house to be built of brick since Roman times, the bricklayers, it is said, being brought from Holland, and it was built to a spectacularly ostentatious design — an almost pyramidical house, its steeply sloping roof peppered with dormer windows, clumped with groups of amazingly tall chimneys, and crowned at the top with a cupola. It was a wonder of the age: fashionable visitors came to stare at it, local people thought it had been built by the Devil, but it was demolished by Gabriele Piozzi, husband of Dr Johnson's friend Mrs Thrale Piozzi, who used its materials to build himself a more convenient mansion nearby. All that is left is the princely stable block, and the abiding legend of The Pyramid House.

from *The Matter of Wales* (1984)

Erddig Restored
Merlin Waterson

My first visit to Erddig was on a dreary February afternoon in 1971. Half a century had not mellowed the harsh Ruabon brick of the suburbs of Wrexham. Although the lodge at the entrance to the park was derelict and roofless except for a few tiles clinging to its gable ends, a Wrexham Scout troop still had its name in large, unruly letters over the entrance porch. The gate piers ended, not in ball finials, but in the jagged stone of their broken necks. Puddles clustered around the gates, which were loosely secured with rusty chain.

Inside the park, the road disintegrated into a ridge of mud flanked by almost continuous potholes. It led down a steep bank, threaded its way between massive exposed tree roots, across a valley of water-meadows, then climbed a hillside of hanging beech woods before emerging abruptly at the house. Fresh white paint on the iron railings leading up to the main door drew attention to the weeds sprouting between the steps and to the variegations of black staining and pale sandstone of the entrance front. Where the shutters of a few of the ground floor rooms were open, reflections quivered in the exquisite imperfections of the old glass. But most of the shutters were closed, many of the windows broken and whole sashes were missing. It was the death mask of a house which faced the two vast slag heaps in the park.

Few park monuments are as telling as those two colliery tips. Erddig was undermined during the 1940s and 1950s and subsidence all but wrecked the house irrevocably. It was scarcely surprising that the National Trust's committees should have baulked at taking on a building that had fallen 5 feet at one end, 3 feet 6 inches at the other, and where a hasty arrangement of pit props in the State Bedroom supported those sections of the ceiling which had not already collapsed: or that the director of a leading national museum should have dismissed Erddig as an 'evil house', which the Trust would be crazy to try to save. But in March 1973 craziness prevailed.

Four years later the house was opened to the public by the Prince of Wales. There were radio and television programmes about Erddig, *The Times* spoke of a 'masterpiece of restoration' and the *Daily Mirror* gave its front page to a picture of the Prince falling off an Erddig penny-farthing. That the change in the house's fortunes should have been so dramatic was not entirely out of character. Since the eighteenth century the Yorke family had delighted in amateur theatricals. The placid, slow-moving middle acts of the drama contrasted strikingly with these melodramatic last scenes of near disaster and triumph.

from *The Servant's Hall* (1980)

A Lover of Nature
Daniel Owen

I had always been a lover of nature and I was never happier than when tramping through the fields and woods gathering nuts, bird nesting, catching trout in the Alun, or if it were summer-time, basking in the sun watching the sky lark ascending into the blue sky from the clover field, and listening to its enchanting song. Many were the afternoons that I spent on the banks of the old river looking at its water flowing incessantly, as it still does today in the same old way. The alder trees continue to grow on its banks. I knew every turn in the river for miles, and I knew all the places where the blackbird and the misselthrush nested in its willow and alder trees. In those days, catching a water-hen or a water-rat, or destroying a wasp's nest, interested me much more than a general election. I could claim to know every chaffinch and warbler in the neighbourhood. I risked my life on two occasions to destroy a crow's nest. Dogs, horses, cattle, wild pigeons and owls fascinated me.

from *Gwen Tomos* (1894) trans. T. Ceiriog Williams & E.R. Harries

People

Many Miles Astray
Evelyn Waugh

In the afternoon I went for a walk and discovered that besides the sea, the railway and the quarry there are some mountains. It is a highly geological country. Everyone in Wales has black spittle and whenever he meets you he says 'borra-da' and spits. I was frightened at first, but after a time I became accustomed to it. Also I discovered that everyone's manners are so good that when you say 'Am I going the right way to Llandulas?' they always say 'yes'. This courtesy has led me many miles astray'.

from *The Journals of Evelyn Waugh* (1976)

The Welsh Type
Beatrix Potter

I could not exactly determine what distinguished the Welsh type, but it is marked, particularly among the women and girls; something about the forehead, eyes, and the fall of the nose, and a rather vacant mouth, a perfect mouse-face sometimes. They all wrinkle up their eyes as though in a strong light, the eyebrows usually arched, the forehead round and the nose long. Dark or blue eyes, red or black hair, an occasional fair, fat type, rather idiotic.

There appear to be many extremely old persons in spite of starved looks. The only well-grown man I saw was the Gamekeeper, a jovial lively party who went about with a big stick looking for poachers. They net the river, steal the scanty game and commit petty thefts in spite of the solemn warning of John Evans's notice boards, 'Who ever will be found taking watercress out of this pond shall be prosecuted'.

There are no shutters to the house for serious crime, but a farmer who overturned in his gig was picked up by the market people, but a considerable sum of loose money which rolled from his pockets was not forthcoming.

The race is said to be deteriorated by much intermarriage. The Denbigh Asylum seemed populous. I thought it very singular that the lunatics should walk in the Park and come up to the garden-railings.

I saw a party of perhaps twenty, with keepers, which I at first took for a cricket match. My aunt seemed to consider the old women amusing. One had appeared and stopped to tea in the servant's-hall. There is a standing reward of five shillings for strayed ones, not worth the risk in my opinion. A man had knocked at the back door and much bewildered Polly by talking about Mr. Gladstone. He fortunately took himself off and presently the keeper arrived in search of him.

Another individual, described as very dangerous and prepared to kill anybody, got into Miss Foster's garden, and being after dark could not be found, so a watch was set in the house, and the following morning he was found sitting among the potatoes, very damp.

These pleasing incidents were scattered over several years, but in my opinion they constitute a drawback to the neighbourhood. I should not care to live amongst the same natives either, it is an uncomfortable, suspicious state when so few can understand English.

from *The Journals of Beatrix Potter: 1881-1897* (1966)

The Llanabba Silver Band
Evelyn Waugh

Picking their way carefully among the dry patches in the waterlogged drive, they reached the playing-fields. Here the haphazard organization of the last twenty-four hours seemed to have been fairly successful. A large marquee was already in position, and Philbrick — still in plus-fours — and three gardeners were at work putting up a smaller tent.

'That's for the Llanabba Silver Band,' said the Doctor.

'Good gracious! Who are these extraordinary-looking people?'

Ten men of revolting appearance were approaching from the drive. They were low of brow, crafty of eye, and crooked of limb. They advanced huddled together with the loping tread of wolves, peering about them furtively as they came, as though in constant terror of ambush; they slavered at their mouths, which hung loosely over their receding chins, while each clutched under his ape-like arm a burden of curious and unaccountable shape. On seeing the Doctor they halted and edged back, those behind squinting and moulting over their companions' shoulders.

'Crikey' said Philbrick. 'Loonies! This is where I shoot.'

'I refuse to believe the evidence of my eyes,' said the Doctor. 'These creatures simply do not exist.'

After brief preliminary shuffling and nudging, an elderly man emerged from the back of the group. He had a rough black beard and wore on his uneven shoulders a druidical wreath of brass mistletoe-berries.

'Why, it's my friend the stationmaster!' said Philbrick

'We are the silver band the Lord bless and keep you,' said the stationmaster in one breath, 'the band that no one could beat whatever but two indeed in the Eisteddfod that for all North Wales was look you.'

'I see,' said the Doctor; 'I see. That's splendid. Well, will you please go into your tent, the little tent over there.'

'To march about you would not like us?' suggested the stationmaster; 'we have a fine yellow flag look you that embroidered for us was in silks.'

'No, no. Into the tent!'

The stationmaster went back to consult with his fellow musicians. There was a baying and growling and yapping as of the jungle at moonrise, and presently he came forward again with an obsequious, sidelong shuffle.

'Three pounds you pay us would you said indeed to at the sports play.'

'Yes, yes, that's right, three pounds. Into the tent!

'Nothing whatever we can play without the money' said the stationmaster firmly.

'How would it be,' said Philbrick, 'if I gave him a clout on the ear?'

'No, no, I beg you to do nothing of the kind. You have not lived in Wales as long as I have.' He took a note-case from his pocket, the sight of which seemed to galvanize the musicians into life; they crowded round, twitching and chattering. The Doctor took out three pound notes and gave them to the stationmaster. 'There you are, Davies!' he said. 'Now take your men into the tent. They are on no account to emerge until after tea; do you understand?'

The band slunk away, and Paul and the Doctor turned back towards the castle.

'The Welsh character is an interesting study,' said Dr Fagan. 'I have often considered writing a little monograph on the subject, but I was afraid it might make me unpopular in the village. The ignorant speak of them as Celts which is of course wholly erroneous. They are of pure Iberian stock — the aboriginal inhabitants of Europe who survive only in Portugal and the Basque district. Celts readily intermarry with their neighbours and absorb them. From the earliest times the Welsh have been looked upon as an unclean people. It is thus that they have preserved their racial integrity. Their sons and daughters rarely mate with human-kind except their own.

from *Decline and Fall* (1929)

For a period of months in 1925 Waugh taught at Arnold House School at Llandulas, near Abergele. When he wrote *Decline and Fall* a few years later it is fair to assume that he drew, to some extent, on his recollections of his period in Clwyd.

Asking a Stallion

Gutun Owain

From Sion ap Rhisiart, Abbot of Valle Crucis, on behalf of his nephew, Maredudd ap Gruffudd

Sion, the companion of saints,
Free-giver, lord of presents,
Son of Richard, having liege
And mastery of knowledge:
Edwin you are, whose feast is
In goodly Valle Crucis;
Like Derfel, in Rhiwfelen
The old Cross yet hallows men:
Your courtiers in heaven share,
A blest host by the river,
While, to your feast, the Godhead
Mercy's complement hath led.
St Martin's grace is yours, Sion,
Your breed is of Rhiwabon;
Your wine, a freer giving
Than of barons or of king!

And I who am your nephew,
Share that ancestry with you.
Meredith, son of Griffith —
Through our sires we're kin and kith —
Ednyfed's stock, and Ierwerth's,
Flowering out of Nannau's worth.

Lord of Yale, I crave a boon,
Ask, without fear, this stallion:
A strong, thin-maned beast is he,
That turns a wolf when angry;
White upon his mouth, foam spills.
His head askew, closed nostrils,
Eyes of wild ox in his head,
Gleam of glass, and mouse-coated;
Gown that's on his breast would be
As fine-edged as I'd fancy;
To the reins, like a great bear's,
Or ox yoked, work his withers:
A hedge the height of a man
He'll clear, if swift the horseman;
He'll leap, to ride an errand,
Every stride an acre of land;
A wild roebuck up the slopes,
A stag to skim the hedgetops;
Clods the full breadth of his shoe
He punches from a meadow —
Four turfs tossed behind his head
As though a boar stampeded.
If, like Samuel, he rides fast,
With fire his road is broadcast:
From nails along the highway
Sparks as from an anvil play:
About him, the flames glisten
Like a steel-hearth in Milan.
Like Taliesin, my lord Sion,
I've come to ask your stallion.
Lord of three fearless tenures,
Maelor, Chirk and Yale are yours.
Your warrior on a war-horse
I'll be, if I get this horse.

Three lives and more may you have
For this horse, in St Asaph.

Gutun Owen (1460-1500) trans. Tony Conran

Mystic Enchantment
John Cowper Powys

Owen's presence affected him with the tremulous heart-beating feeling such a young savage might experience who finds that the god of his race-upon whose rough image he had long cast a negligent and even critical eye — has suddenly appeared to him in the wistful and helpless beauty of his real identity — out of that familiar and neglected shrine. It was partly the scrupulous delicacy of the man's forked beard and of the thin gold thread round the brow that evoked this feeling, for in some curious way these details bore an infinitely pathetic look, as if the figure thus adorned and tended had been prepared or had prepared himself for some mysterious sacrificial rite.

Rhisiart never again got quite the impression he received that midsummer afternoon, and there came moments when its memory grew blurred. But it never altogether left him; and the Owen he saw that day took his place, easily, naturally and with a fatal inevitableness, on the ramparts of Dinas Bran and gathered into himself their mystic enchantment.

from *Owain Glendower* (1941)

Katherine of Berain
A.G. Bradley

What has chiefly made her famous is the fact, not only of her having had four husbands, all celebrities, but also of the humours which surround their overtures. For the first was a Salusbury of Lleweni, by whom she became the mother of the lion-killing and tree-uprooting 'Syr John,' and the grandmother of the goodly flock we saw upon his tomb at Whitchurch. But in no long time death granted to this notable lady what we can only assume she regarded as a happy release, seeing the fashion in which she outraged what we should now at any rate regard as the most elementary-proprieties. Now, it seems to have been the right thing in those days for a widow, when following her husband's body to the grave, to have been conducted thither by one or other of her lamented consort's friends. The right of offering consolation and drying the lady's tears on this solemn occasion fell to Sir Richard Clough, a sober widower of much wealth and great renown. Sir Richard dried them with a vengeance; for before they reached the church, he had offered himself as his deceased friend's successor, and had been actually accepted. Whether Maurice Wynn, of Gwydir, one of the foremost gentlemen in Wales, and also a mourner, was hurried by any suspicion of what might be going on into action almost as precipitate, or whether with a little more sense of decency than his rival, he had already laid his plans for the return journey, history does not say. But it fell to his lot to escort the sorrowing widow home again, and great was his consternation, and deep his chagrin when he discovered that, prompt and timely though it was, his offer came too late. He did, however, the best thing that under the circumstances was possible; and the lady rose to the occasion and promised him most solemnly the reversion of her hand should she have to perform the same sad ceremony over Sir Richard as she had just completed over her first husband. Maurice Wynn was something of a philosopher no doubt, and had already buried two wives at Gwydir, and, possessing his soul in patience, he reaped in due time his just reward, and won his third. For Sir Richard, died at forty; and the gracious Catherine being once more free, proved true to her troth, and went to preside over one of the stateliest households and fairest estates in Wales. This, however, is by no means the end of the story, for she buried Maurice Wynn also, and not only that, but made a fourth venture with Edward Thelwall, of Plas-y-Ward. Never surely was there such a record made by a woman of quality. Herself of royal descent and great possessions, and by all accounts of singular mental attraction, if not surpassing beauty, she married successively into four of the most powerful houses of North Wales.

Her descendants are so numerous that almost every family of position, and many no doubt of no longer any at all, in North Wales boast or could boast descent from her, and she shares with the fertile island of Anglesea the sobriquet of Mam Cymru, or Mother of Wales.

from *Highways and Byways of North Wales* (1898)

Humphrey Llwyd
John Parry

Humphrey Llwyd had four children, two sons and two daughters. One of the former, named Henry, settled at Cheam in Surrey, and his great grandson, the Rev. Robert Lloyd, who was rector of St. Paul's, Covent Garden made an unsuccessful effort to claim the Barony of Lumley in right of the sister of Lord Lumley, who, as already mentioned, was married to the subject of this memoir. Whether any descendants of the family be now living, we have not been able to ascertain.

Of the character and habits of Humphrey Llwyd we have but few traces beyond what his works supply. Camden, who immediately followed him in the literary world, or was rather his contemporary, describes him as standing pre-eminent in that branch of antiquarian research, to which he had devoted himself. The writer of his life in the 'Athensae Oxonienses' represents him besides, as a 'person of great eloquence, an excellent rhetorician, and a sound philosopher'. With these qualifications, of themselves sufficient for his fame, he united the fashionable accomplishments of the age, and was, in particular as we have seen, well skilled in music, which often proved, during his latter years, the solace of those hours that were snatched from the labours of study, or the duties of his profession. It was, we may presume, the dulce læon of all his cares. In his person, if we may judge from a portrait of him still in existence, he was peculiarly gifted, while the manly beauty of his countenance indicated the corresponding intelligence of his mind.

The several literary productions of Humphrey Llwyd have already been specified; but it may be proper to offer a few more remarks on those relating to Wales. Among this number the 'History of Cambia' has been the most generally read, and is, accordingly, the most popular. It is founded, as is well known, on the Welsh chronicle of Caradog of Llancarvon. It was left in an unfinished state by the author. . .

The 'Fragment of the Description of Britain' embraces a geographical and antiquarian view of the whole island, as well as a cursory account of its existing condition, according to its three divisions of England, Scotland, and Wales, and is remarkable for the boldness with which the author controverts some received authorities respecting the sites of several ancient fortresses and towns. This seems to have been a work of great research, not fewer than sixty-eight authors, native and foreign, being cited in the course of it. It was first printed at Cologne in 1572; and in the following year an English translation by Twyne, accompanied by several copies of commendatory verses was published under the title of the 'Breviary of Britain'. Moses Williams too, an able Welsh antiquary, printed, in 1723, a handsome edition of the original work with annotations. The following specimen of the publication, extracted from Twyne's translation, may not be out of place here. It is a passage, in which the author describes the place of his birth, with reference to its state at the time he wrote. 'This fine town', he says, 'and my sweet country, being compassed well nigh about with very fair parks, and standing in the entrance of an exceeding pleasant valley, aboundeth plentifully with all things that are necessary to the use of man. The hills yield flesh and white meats. The most fertile valley very good corn and grass. The sweet rivers, with the sea at hand, minister all sorts of fish and fowl. Strange wines come thither forth of Spain, France, and Greece abundantly. And being the chief town of the shire, standing in the very middle of the country, it is a great market town, famous, and much frequented with wares and people from all parts of North Wales. The indwellers have the use of both tongues, and, being endued by Kings of England with many privileges and liberties, are ruled by their own laws'.

from *The Cambrian Plutarch* (1834)

Self Restraint
Lord Herbert of Cherbury

After I had attained the age of nine, during all which time I lived in my grandmother's house at Eyrton, my parents thought fit to send me to some place where I might learn the Welsh tongue, as believing it necessary for me to treat with my friends and tenants who understood no other language. Whereupon I was recommended to Mr. Edward Thelwal of Plas y ward, in Denbighshire. This gentleman, I must remember with honour, as having of himself acquired the most exact knowledge of Greek, Latin, French, Italian, and Spanish, and all other learning, having for that purpose neither gone beyond seas, nor so much as had the benefit of any university. Besides he was of that rare temper in governing his choler, that I never saw him angry during the time of my stay there, and have heard the same of him many years before. When occasion of offence was given him, I have seen him redden in the face, and after remain for a time silent, but when he spake his words were so calm and gentle that I found he had digested his choler; yet, I confess I could never obtain that perfection, as being subject to passion and choler more than I ought, and generally, to speak my mind freely, sought rather to imitate those who, having fire within doors, chose rather to give it vent than suffer it to burn the house. I commend much more the manner of Mr. Thelwal; and certainly he that can forbear speaking for some while will remit much of his passion.

from *Autobiography* (1624)

The Welshness of Judge Jeffreys
H.B. Irving

It must not be forgotten that 'Judge Jeffreys' was a Welshman. Matthew Arnold has described wit, vivacity, an audacious love of excitement, a want of measure and steadfastness and sanity, as prevailing characteristics of the Celtic nature. Lord Justice Vaughan Williams has added disregard of personal liberty. These qualities have been for some time associated in the public mind with 'Judge Jeffreys.' Amidst the Teutonic moderation of his immediate relatives, it may not be unreasonable to regard George as a wilful protest on the part of the Celtic element in the family character against threatened extinction.

At Acton Park, in a beautiful green corner of the county of Denbighshire, near the town of Wrexham, George Jeffreys was born in the year 1648. Acton Park had been the family seat for a considerable period. Descended from a long line of distinguished ancestors, the house of Jeffreys could claim to be one of the oldest families among the gentry of Wales.

The father whose son was destined to dissipate so rudely the unpretentious merit of the family achievement was Mr. John Jeffreys. He had proved no alien to the honourable traditions of his house; and, at the age of eighty-four, when 'Judge Jeffreys' had ceased to be anything but a hated name, this sturdy old gentleman felt justified in blessing God 'that he had always studied the welfare and happiness of his children, and had never been guilty of an unkind or unjust act to any of them'. He had chosen a fitting wife in Margaret Ireland. This lady was the daughter of Sir Thomas Ireland, a Lancashire gentleman, erstwhile a Serjeant-at-law and learned editor of *Coke's Reports*. Mrs. Jeffreys was a pious good woman, if we are to believe the testimony of her friend Philip Henry, the eminent Dissenter, and one who did her best to bring up her children in a godly fashion. There is some reason for believing that Jeffreys's parents were themselves Dissenters, and it may well be that George's bringing up was unpleasantly austere to a child of his temperament. At any rate, it is admissible to suggest that in his early training and the religious tone of his father's household, Jeffreys found a primary cause for the lively hatred he evinced in later years towards the non-conformists. It must not also be forgotten that Jeffreys' earliest years, 1648-1660, were passed during the period of Puritan ascendancy, a period no doubt trying in many respects to vivacious children.

from *The Life of Judge Jeffreys* (1898)

The Gypsy Girl
Augustus John

While staying with John Sampson at Bettws-gwrgil-goch, Innes and I one day set out for the neighbouring town of Corwen. In the bar of an inn we came across a family of gypsies with whom we consorted. This family was of the rare tribe of Florence. One of the young women, Udina, was of great beauty, elegance and charm. All gypsy girls are flirts and this one was no exception to the rule. Uninured to their wiles, Innes no less than I was deeply moved; we both secretly established an understanding with Udina. The family, were to depart next day for Ruthyn. At length, reluctantly, we said good night and returned to Sampson's. The next morning Innes was not to be found. I guessed his whereabouts. As it turned out, stealing a march on me, he had risen early and gone back to Corwen to rejoin the Florences, but finding them gone had set out to overtake them on foot. On the outskirts of Ruthyn, overcome with fatigue, to which the state of his health no doubt contributed, he had fallen by the road-side, and was discovered in collapse by a charitable passer-by who took him home, and kept him in bed till he recovered. But Udina Florence, the girl of both our dreams, was never seen again.

from *Chiaroscuro* (1952)

A Bushel of Chaff
John Ceiriog Hughes

When I was a young lad, no pleasure was higher
Than whittling and chipping before my dad's fire,
While sister sat knitting and Mam evermore
Was spinning, was spinning upon the stone floor
Come what may come now,
Man that I am now,
Eagerly I'm flying
On the wings of longing
Back once more
To the cosy, unassuming old homestead that I knew.

When I was a shepherd at Hafod y Rhyd
At hayfield and cornfield my sheep came to feed.
In shade of an oaktree by collie I'd lie
And dozing and drowsy how happy was I.
Look as I may now,
Where I may stray now,
There are my affections
With my recollection
Of those fields
Enjoying the meadows all summer's livelong day.

The swallow must wander from home in the eaves
But next Spring returns to the nest it now leaves;
And we too must wander, again and again
Remembering the old home that nurtured us then.
Troubles are heavy,
Bitter life's story
But let who'll be bitter,

Sweet yet to remember
My white home
In the glow of inspiration that is smiling on me still.

1886: trans. Tony Conran

Twm o'r Nant
Sir Leonard Twiston Davies & Averyl Edwards

He, like so many figures in Welsh literature, was self-taught and came of working parentage; his father and mother were country people and his nicknames 'Tom o' the Brook' and 'Tom o' the Dingle' are indicative of his free surroundings. One bright summer he had three weeks schooling, and instead of bewailing this unexpected imprisonment, he applied himself with desperate energy to the task of reading and spelling, and did actually master the putting together of a few words. This inspired him with a longing to write, and, using elderberry juice for ink, he traced all the words he knew on the margin of any book he could lay hands on. But a windfall came his way: the village shop caught fire, and amongst the damaged articles were a number of sheets of paper only scorched at the edges, which his mother bought for a penny and sewed together to make him writing-books. The local blacksmith wrote him out a copy of the alphabet, and in his own words, from this beginning, he 'went on getting paper and ink and something to copy now from this person, and now from that, until I learned to read Welsh and to write it at the same time.' When he was ten years old, he made a valuable friend in the person of the old chapel-reader of Pentre Foelas, who had quite a library of ancient books which he was allowed to borrow. He had already written a couple of interludes, and at the age of twelve he wrote one founded on Bunyan's *Spiritual Courtship.* This masterpiece was stolen by another lad, and the loss, together with his parent's disapproval of his literary efforts, greatly discouraged him. But after a while a new interlude was produced and entrusted to a local poet, who actually sold it for ten shillings to the youths of the district, for them to act the following summer. Twm himself obtained no more profit, 'save a sup of ale from the players.' Folk plays or interludes, which began in the fifteenth century to supersede the moralities and mystery plays of an earlier age, were immensely popular with the country people. Thomas Edwards, to give him his baptismal name, has been eulogized as the Shakespeare of Wales, a comparison grotesquely wide of the mark; but one trait he possessed in common with the master an extraordinary zest for handling the materials of everyday life. The country people, their births, their deaths, their loves, their hates, the savagery of that rough age, poverty and plenty, feastings and mournings, all were woven by him into his ballads and folk plays, but his characters are 'puppets' who come to life only by the jerking of strings. He himself describes his love of writing as 'a madness and wildness — for rhyming and poetising a rage for singing and satyrizing everything he saw going on;' and he adds that it was a wonder that he was not killed by some of the victims of his sharp tongue. On the contrary, he nearly destroyed another lad who had dared to argue with him, and the following day, a rumour being raised that his victim was dead, he 'escaped across the mountain to Pentre Foelas to the old man Simon Dafydd to read his old books.'

After his marriage, at the age of twenty-four, he and his country wife took a little holding just outside Denbigh. They kept three cows and four horses: the last helped Tom to learn his living as a wood carter. Misfortune came upon him: three of the horses died, and he got into debt from which he extricated himself by writing and playing an interlude for some miners in Flintshire. Another interlude *Riches and Poverty* brought him considerable profit, and for the next twelve years he divided his time between interlude writing and wood carting. At the end of this period he had saved three hundred pounds, no mean fortune for a country man of eighteenth-century Wales; but he went bail for a relative who failed and left him with a load of debt, the burden of which became so intolerable that Twm was forced to flee from county to county to escape his creditors. During this unfortunate period the playwright became turnpike-keeper, but his imagination was in no way blunted, and with a Welshman's vision he beheld ghostly hearses and coaches driving through his toll-gate at dead of night; one indeed, he declared, passed through the gate while it was shut and 'I saw . . . the wheels scattering the stones in the road.'

In the intervals of playwriting he traded next as a stonemason and a bricklayer, becoming, according to his own proud boast, 'a very lion at bricklaying.'

When he was in sight of his sixtieth birthday a neighbour taunted him by declaring that he had noticed a weakening of his physical powers. Tom's answer was to carry, as one load, three sacks of wheat, containing three bushels each, from the hall of the 'Hand' Inn at Ruthyn out into the street and back again.

Borrow describes how he went to visit the ruins of the abbey where the great Welsh poet, Iolo Goch, lies buried, and how an old countrywoman invited him into her cottage and, on learning his quest, exclaimed: 'Iolo Goch! I have never heard of him but if you want a poet I can show you the picture of one,' and she brought forth a print of Twm o'r Nant, proudly adding: 'He is called the Shakespeare of Wales.' The couplet under the print ran thus:

> Llun Gwr yw llawn gwir Awen;
> Y Byd a lanwodd o'i Ben.
>
> God in his head the Muse instill'd
> And from his head the world he fill'd.

The work of Twm, rough and untutored as it is, is yet an invaluable mirror of his times. The frequent doggerel and the faulty metre is shot through and through with that natural genius which held enthralled the companions who listened to his interludes. The very breath of that vanished age stirs the pages as his great procession of characters, hat-makers, cloggers, cobblers, ballad-mongers, jailers, hangmen, shopkeepers, and beggars pass before the reader. Keen humour and satirical criticism characterized his work: 'the Swift of Welsh literature' is at least nearer the mark than the 'Shakespeare of Wales." Before the Methodists set their faces against all play acting, his interludes driving home a sound moral, despite the frequent impropriety of their language exercised a profound influence on the country people for whom they were written.

from *Welsh Life in the Eighteenth Century* (1939)

A Visit to Pennant

Richard Warner

I walked to Downing, the seat of Mr. Pennant, about three miles from Holywell, who had ratified me by an invitation to his house, the seat of virtue, kindness, and benevolence, as well as literature, science, and taste. The walk is agreeable, and diversified, particularly towards the mansion, to which I approached by a rural path, winding through a beautiful well-wooded dingle.

Downing, though not the original seat of this respectable family, is a house of some antiquity, as the date 1627 in the front of it evinces. Its plan is judicious and commodious, and the situation, like that of all the rural residences of our ancestors is low, sequestered, and sheltered. The little valley, in the bottom of which it stands, is formed by two finely-swelling hills, that rise to the east and west, covered with the dark umbrage of venerable woods; but which, sinking into a sweeping depression towards the north, admit a fine view of the Chester channel. Much taste is displayed in the laying out of the small but beautiful garden ground; where a judicious management, and an agreeable variety, give the appearance of considerably greater extent to this little paradise than it really lays claim to.

To see the 'literary veteran' by whom the public has been so much amused, and so much instructed, in the peaceful shades of his own academical bowers, spending the close of an honourable and useful life in active beneficence, crowned with the blessings of the poor, and the love and esteem of an extensive neighbourhood,would have conveyed to my mind an emotion of unspeakable pleasure, had it not been checked by the appearance of ill health.

form A *Second Walk Through Wales* (1798)

Downing
John Davies

Seventy rasping he lives in the saddlery
of the estate now run out of paths.
He keeps the tv. busy. The past? The brisk squire
who toured the eighteenth century and met Voltaire?
Not interested. But around pleasure garden summer house
Bob Weston cleared gullies for parched ironworks
lopped trees in the dingles was tolerant it seems
of poachers. The house burned down as an insurance job
is a DIY kit. Its drive can't find the gateway.
Tunnels though and waterways built by miners

are intact theirs or land's revenge on stateliness
where ponds sag under weed.

Below on Mostyn sands cockles have been found
by diggers in balaclavas linked to the underground economy.
Jobs, they're rare as oysters. Unmarked trucks
sidled, and from dunes. they say the DHSS took photos.
Bob Weston's watched — Dunkirk again, another
scramble grab what you can then home the brass
will know the score. Except the brass aren't on your side.

Now that it's wanted for caravans, what no one could visit
is lamented. People will flood in, there'll be petitions.
But he'll not be collecting who likes that brand new
pub at the junction and leaves his dog at home.

from *Flight Patterns* (1991)

The Williams Wynns
A.H. Dodd

The first Sir Watkin Williams Wynn (1692-1749) was a pillar of Welsh Jacobitism, a doughty opponent of Walpole both in the House and in the country, and an intrepid fox-hunter: something of a Squire Western in fact. His successor, who came of age in 1770 was of a different complexion. His hobby was the stage and he built at Wynnstay a theatre in which he and his neighbours and his household servants (some of them chosen for their histrionic talent) performed to select audiences of the neighbouring gentry. The supreme moment of his life came when David Garrick himself paid a visit to one of the performances. The third Sir Watkin succeeded to the estate at the beginning of the French Revolution, and once again a new order was inaugurated. The third Sir Watkin was instrumental in founding the Wrexham Agricultural Society, and ten years later the Wynnstay theatre was dismantled and appropriated to the uses of an agricultural meeting. Henceforth a great show of sheep and cattle was held each year at Wynnstay, with prizes for good farming, and a Gargantuan feast where five or six hundred guests discussed crops and manures and drank appropriate toasts. Only when Sir Watkin was away on military service, and on a few later occasions when circumstances proved unfavourable was this popular institution suspended and the presence of Coke of Holkham at one of the meetings made the baronet as happy as his father had been when he inveigled Garrick to Wynnstay. He was less successful in his attempt to introduce the culture of hops into Denbighshire and his efforts to improve the breed of Merioneth cattle by the introduction of Highland bulls were defeated by the refusal of the beasts to take kindly to farm life but his extensive afforestation of lands round Llangollen gained him the gold medal of the Society of Arts.

from *The Industrial Revolution in North Wales* (1933)

Pastoral

Emyr Humphreys

This morning, yawning, Dic Fawr said
'Evans the "Ship and Castle" is dead'
'Is he indeed ? Poor chap,' I said.

The huge horse rose in its shadowy stall
We smoked and watched its brown excreta fall
And Dic, said, spitting 'After all

You couldn't expect a chap like that
With bottles to hand from where he sat
Not to soak. His belly was like a vat.'

Dic went across to stir the horse's feed.
'Come on, Eat up,' he said, 'you're harrowing the fifteen acre field
All day today,' and wistfully to me, 'It was a nice death indeed.'

Outside the lark was gargling with dew
When Dic led out Captain Bell and True
The sunlight dripped in the lane. The sky was blue.

from *Ancestor Worship* (1970)

An Indelible Mark on the Soul

David Jones

My father was born in 1860 in Treffynnon and spent his childhood and youth in that town of Gwenfrewi's Well. It is odd to recall that before his coming of age, and totally unknown to his 'world of Wales' or the world of England either, in the Tremeirchion area not so very many miles to the west, a 'man in black' entranced by the particular characteristics of Welsh metric was at his labours which were destined within half a century to have a very decided effect on English *poiesis*. The mere idea would have seemed as impossible in Sir Fflint as it would have seemed preposterous and outrageous to *The Times* newspaper.

Governmental English opinion and anglophile Welsh opinion in the eighteen-sixties and seventies are sufficiently well known, so that the suggestion that this Brittonic tongue, 'the main obstacle to civilization in Wales', could ever, under any circumstances, be a vivifying influence on English poetic forms would have appeared not much less absurd than to suggest a revival and vivification of *yr iaith Gymraeg* itself.

But we all tend to suppose of something or other that we think long since ploughed-in and forgot that 'the dew on him did fall . . . and Barleycorn stood up again and that surprised them all!'

My grandfather, John Jones, and I think his wife also, were natives of Ysgeifiog, which place is on or very near the presumed alignment of Clawdd Offa. I say presumed because while that remarkable earthwork is fully evident to archaeologists some miles to the south and picks up again nearer the coast, there is a gap in the evidence in the Ysgeifiog area of Tegeingl. I write from a Nursing Home and so am without the requisite maps and references, so write as my memory serves. But John Jones, Ysgeifiog, has always been associated in my mind with the great vallum of the Mercian King in the 8th century, which looks one way toward the Welsh heartland and its hills and thick wooded valley-ways, and beyond to the heights of Arfon herself, while the other way, looking east lay the flats and richer soil of what was to become shire-land of the Mercian — deep-furrowed of the coulter, wider the share's furrow of the heavy English plough-beam.

It appears John Jones, Ysgeifiog, although totally Welsh in blood, and who habitually conversed with his wife in the native tongue, discouraged, as far as he could, the use of Welsh in his eldest son, my father. His other children appear to have used either tongue as they chose. It is easy to see the intention of John Jones, it was to make his eldest son as fully English-speaking as may be. How else 'get on' in the world?

It may seem a very far cry from the great border families such as the Vaughans or the Herberts in the reign of Elizabeth the First to the humble families of farming stock or craftsmen of the Clwyd or Dee in the reign of Victoria, but their motives were not all that dissimilar.

John Jones wished his son to be at no disadvantage in the great world, so the more the lad had command of English, the better. But of course it was impossible to be brought up in Treffynnon in the eighteen-sixties and seventies without an understanding of *yr hen iaith* alongside the speech of 'the children of Ronnwen', the tongue of the burgess breed of 'the daughters of Alis', the tongue of the Realm of our sovereign Lady Victoria.

But was not she 'exalted with the Crown of London', like Bendigeidfran son of Llyr?

Kleio plays her own tricks.

My father knew and could converse in Welsh along with his play-mates, though it may be not with the fluency of his younger sisters and brothers, in that they were, it seems, exempt from any parental discouragement. A curious case of primogeniture, applied to linguistics, in gavelkind-minded Wales.

But I do not know enough of the actual situation to speak with any confidence, but am judging from subsequent fragments of evidence....

My father had come to London in the eighteen-eighties and by the time of my childhood in the first decade of this present century, if his Welsh was greatly eroded, he sang songs to us in Welsh, and the clear-vowelled Cymraeg and perfect pitch without any sign of effort filled me with wonder, certainly with pride, and a kind of awe. He also told us stories current in that north-eastern corner of the Welsh lands from which he had come. It was that sense of 'otherness' that was the heritage he handed on to me.

I have no forgetfulness of being taken for the first time to visit relatives in Gwynedd Wen. Somehow or other we were packed into a hansom, two parents, three small children and much impedimenta, to Euston for the night-train, so it was pitch dark; for most of the journey I was fast asleep and can remember nothing until we were, I suppose, somewhere between Crewe and Chester, anyway it was, I think, light, but I was told to go to sleep again as there was a long way to go. Somewhere west of Chester I was again wide awake, and my father was saying, 'Well, here you are now, or will be in a few moments'. I looked one way and the coastal flats of the wide estuary of the Dee stretched to the taut line of the sea-horizon. I looked the other way along the *morlan* to the rising contours of the hills and far beyond them in the morning light the misted heights, now lost, now found, away to the fastnesses of Gwynedd Uchaf. Though of course I had not yet heard that term. But the Rubicon had been passed. And so this was the land of which my father had so often spoken and that's why he had said just then, 'Well, here you are now'.

This was at least the first glimpse of a visual 'otherness' and for me it was an otherness that, as is said of certain of the sacraments, is not patient of repetition, but leaves an indelible mark on the soul of us.

A letter to *Poetry Wales* (1972)

Three Colourful Characters

'Nimrod' (Charles James Apperley)

Our neighbourhood abounded in what are called 'characters.' For example: where would now be found another Tom Eyton (pronounced Eaton) of the Mount, so called because the house, although situated in the town of Wrexham, was placed on an ascent, and approached by a flight of steps? This gentleman was in appearance a true specimen of the old English squire of those days, a stamp then fast wearing away. But what a bundle of prejudices was he! Fancy his refusing to dine at any man's house where he was not certain of finding a batter pudding so hard that it might have been tossed over the roof without spoiling its form; and a certain description of wine-glass — a very small one, perhaps twenty to a bottle — which would enable him to drink a bumper to every toast. Although I was young when he died, I have a perfect recollection of 'Old Tom Eyton', as he was always called, on his cropped brown gelding, which he considered a hunter, but which would not now be thought fast enough for one of our fast mails. I, however, used to look upon his owner as a prodigy, having been told that he occasionally would ride over a five-barred gate at what is called a standing jump the time occupied by the said standing jump being as much as would enable a modern hunter to leap a gate and cross half a large field into the bargain. Still old Tom Eyton was a gentleman in every sense of the word; and despite his bumper toasts, cut not his stick until the sap that nourished it was dried up by all-withering old age.

And how plainly have I before my eyes his next-door neighbour, the Doctor Meredith — pronounced by the vulgar, Me-reddith. The doctor was the younger of two brothers, of very ancient family; and having luckily an independent fortune, his practice was extremely limited. I say luckily, because it is my opinion that practically he knew no more of the healing art than I myself do. But it was far from his wish to be considered in that light; and with this view he not only appeared in church booted and spurred, with whip in his hand ready for a start, but would often be called out by his servant, as if a case of emergency awaited his immediate aid. The doctor's weak side, indeed, was his vanity: nothing pleased him more than to be consulted by any young friend, from whom he would never take a fee, but an invitation to dinner would be the result. I often made one of a party of young men of the neighbourhood at the doctor's hospitable board; and the awful state of drunkenness in which we usually left him might be better imagined than described.

Johnny Wynne of Ryton was a fine specimen of the highest class of English yeomen; and a yeoman did he call himself, although able to purchase a regiment of esquires of the present day. Moreover, from his quiet kind demeanour, he was admitted into the society of the neighbourhood, being often a guest at Wynnstay, Emral, and other houses of note. But what rare accomplishments had Johnny Wynne, to suit the taste of my younger days, in the neighbourhood in which he lived? He could drink two-and-thirty half-pints (two gallons) of ale at a sitting! and had any one chanced to pass his house at six o'clock the next morning, he would have found him up and stirring, as though nothing unusual with him had occurred! Then how well he rode to hounds on his little black gelding, which he called 'Everlasting', and which he rode for nearly twenty years without missing a season! The late Lord Forester said he was the best man to scramble over a country that he ever met with, and was used to speak with delight of one feat performed by him in his presence. He rode at a fence and landed in a marl-pit, losing his hat and wig in the scramble. He very coolly re-entered the pit, and swimming towards his lost head-gear, first brought out the hat in his teeth, and next the wig.

from *My Life and Times,* edited by E.D. Cumming, 1927)

Dirty Williams
Robert Graves

One or two random memories remain of this training period at Wrexham. The landlord of my billet, a Welsh solicitor, greatly overcharged us though pretending amicability. He wore a wig — or, to be more exact, three wigs, with hair of progressive lengths. After wearing the medium-sized hair for a few days, he would put on the long-haired wig, and say that, dear him! he really ought to get a hair-cut. Then he would leave the house and, in a public lavatory perhaps, or a wayside copse, change into the short-haired wig, which he wore until he thought time to change to the medium once more. The deception came to light when one of the officers billeted with me got drunk and raided his bedroom. This officer, a Williams, was an extreme example of the sly Border Welshman. The drunker he became, the more shocking his confessions. He told me once about a Dublin girl whom he had promised to marry, and even slept with on the strength of a diamond engagement ring. 'Only paste, really,' he boasted. The day before the wedding she lost a foot — cut off by a Dalkey tram, and he hurriedly left Dublin. 'But, Graves, she was a lovely, lovely girl until that happened!' Williams had been a medical student at Trinity College, Dublin. Whenever he visited Chester, the nearest town, to pick up a prostitute, he would not only appeal to her patriotism to charge him nothing, but always gave my name. I knew of this because these women wrote me reproachful letters. At last I told him in the mess: 'In future you are going to be distinguished from all the other Williamses in the regiment by being called 'Dirty Williams'. The name stuck. By one shift or another he escaped all trench-service, except for a short spell in a quiet sector, and lasted the war out safely.

Goodbye to All That (1929)

Rural Poverty
T. Gwynn Jones

I owe to my father the ensuing picture of the life of a labourer in the Hiraethog territory over eighty years ago:

'I have often wondered how they managed to live. Wages were low, and paid in kind. My father employed a workman who lived in a small cottage on the farm.

He had a wife and seven or eight children, who grew up to be strong and healthy — the sons were of splendid physique. The family kept a pig and some fowls and were allowed to plant a few rows of potatoes on the farm in return for the manure from the pig-keeping. They also had butter-milk and occasionally some butter free. During the sheep-shearing and the harvest, the mother and the elder children assisted, while the younger played about within sight. I remember seeing the mother going now and again from hay-making to feed an infant left in charge of a little sister. Thus practically throughout the summer the whole family was fed with but slight calls upon its own gains. A fleece or two of wool would be given nominally to the mother, and the children gathered wool from the hedges and brambles, with which material for clothing was provided. During the summer season the children went barefooted. For the winter, the father made clogs for them from our cast-off boots. During the winter season, they lived on bread made of barley mixed with a little wheat, bacon, potatoes, and butter-milk. Peat was burnt for fuel, and in the evenings the father and the elder boys made baskets, wooden spoons and other articles, while the mother and the girls knitted stockings and made simple garments which were sometimes sold to others. Story-telling went on at the same time, as it did at the farm-houses. My own father used to tell stories and sing songs for us when were were very young, but later, having come under the influence of the religious activies of the time, he gave up the practice, considering it to be sinful. When later I became interested in Folklore and prayed him to repeat for me some of his former stories and songs, he refused to comply. Thus, throughout the district, a mass of such material was for ever lost.'

from *Welsh Folklore and Folk Custom* (1929)

An American Eavesdropper
Nathaniel Hawthorne

There was a steep ascent from the commencement of the long street of Ruthin, till I reached the market-place, which is of nearly triangular shape, and an exceedingly old-looking place. Houses of stone or plastered brick; one or two with timber frames; the roofs of an uneven line, and bulging out or sinking in; the slates moss-grown. Some of them have two peaks and even three in a row, fronting on the streets, and there is a stone market-house with a table of regulations. In this market-place there is said to be a stone on which King Arthur beheaded one of his enemies; but this I did not see. All these villages were very lively, as the omnibus drove in; and I rather imagine it was market-day in each of them, — there being quite a bustle of Welsh people. The old women came round the omnibus courtesying and intimating their willingness to receive alms, — witch-like women, such as one sees in pictures or reads of in romances, and very unlike anything feminine in America. Their style of dress cannot have changed for centuries. It was quite unexpected to me to hear Welsh so universally and familiarly spoken. Everybody spoke it. The omnibus driver could speak but imperfect English; there was a jabber of Welsh all through the streets and market-places; and it flowed out with a freedom quite different from the way in which they expressed themselves in English. I had had an idea that Welsh was spoken rather as a freak and in fun than as a native language; it was so strange to find another language the people's actual and earnest medium of thought within so short a distance of England. But English is scarcely more known to the body of the Welsh people than to the peasantry of France. Moreover, they sometimes pretend to ignorance, when they might speak it fairly enough.

from *Passages from the English Notebooks* (1870)

Early Memories
Sir Henry Morton Stanley

One of the first things I remember is to have been gravely told that I had come from London in a band-box, and to have been assured that all babies came from the same place. It satisfied my curiosity for several years as to the cause of my coming; but, later, I was informed that my mother had hastened to her parents from London to be delivered of me; and that, after recovery, she had gone back to the Metropolis, leaving me in the charge of my grandfather, Moses Parry, who lived within the precincts of Denbigh Castle.

Forty years of my life have passed, and this delving into my earliest years appears to me like an exhumation of Pompeii, buried for centuries under the scoriae, lava, and volcanic dust of Vesuvius. To the man of the Nineteenth Century, who paces the recovered streets and byeways of Pompeii, how strange seem the relics of the far distant life! Just so appear to me the little fatherless babe, and the orphaned child.

Up to a certain time I could remember well every incident connected with those days; but now I look at the child with wonder, and can scarcely credit that out of that child I grew. How quaint that bib and tucker, that short frock, the fat legs, the dimpled cheeks, the clear, bright, grey eyes, the gaping wonderment at the sight of a stranger; and I have to brush by the stupefied memories of a lifetime!

When I attempt to arrest one of the fleeting views of those early stages of my life, the foremost image which presents itself is that of my grandfather's house, a white-washed cottage, situated at the extreme left of the Castle, with a long garden at the back, at the far end of which was the slaughterhouse where my Uncle Moses pole-axed calves, and prepared their carcasses for the market; and the next is of myself, in bib and tucker, between grandfather's knees, having my fingers guided, as I trace the alphabet letters on a slate. I seem to hear, even yet, the encouraging words of the old man, 'Thou wilt be a man yet before thy mother, my man of men.'

It was then, I believe, that I first felt what it was to be vain. I was proud to believe that, though women might be taller, stronger, and older than I, there lay a future before me that the most powerful women could never hope to win. It was then also I gathered that a child's first duty was to make haste to be a man, in order that I might attain that highest human dignity.

My grandfather appears to me as a stout old gentleman, clad in corduroy breeches, dark stockings, and long Melton coat, with a clean-shaven face, rather round, and lit up by humorous grey eyes. He and I occupied the top floor, which had an independent entrance from the garden. The lower rooms were inhabited by my uncles, Moses and Thomas. By-and-bye, there came a change. My strong, one-armed Uncle Moses married a woman named Kitty, a flaxen-haired, fair girl of a decided temper; and after that event we seldom descended to the lower apartments.

from *Autobiography*, edited by Dorothy Stanley (1909)

A Surprise Visit
Nathaniel Hawthorne

. . . we set out to walk along the embankment, although the sky looked very threatening. The wind, however, was so strong, and had such a full sweep at us on the top of the bank, that we decided on taking a path that led from it across the moor. But we soon had cause to repent of this; for, which way so ever we turned, we found ourselves cut off by a ditch or a little stream; so that here we were, fairly astray on Rhyddlan moor, the old battle-field of the Saxons and Britons, and across which, I suppose, the fiddlers and mountebanks had marched to the relief of the Earl of Chester. Anon, too, it began to shower; and it was only after various leaps and scramblings that we made our way, to a large farm-house, and took shelter under a cart-shed. The back of the house to which we gained access was very dirty and ill kept; some dirty children peeped at us as we approached, and nobody had the civility to ask us in; so we took advantage of the first cessation of the shower to resume our way. We were shortly overtaken by a very intelligent-looking and civil man, who seemed to have come from Rhyddlan, and, said he was going to Rhyl. We followed his guidance over stiles and along hedge-row paths which we never could have threaded rightly by ourselves.

By-and-by our kind guide had to stop at an intermediate farm, but he gave us full directions how to proceed, and we went on till it began to shower again pretty briskly, and we took refuge in a little bit of old stone cottage, which, small as it was, had a greater antiquity than any mansion in America. The door was open, and as we approached, we saw several children gazing at us; and their mother, a pleasant-looking woman, who seemed rather astounded at the visit that was about to befall her, tried to draw a tattered curtain over part of her interior, which she fancied even less fit to be seen than the rest. To say the truth, the house was not at all better than a pigsty; and while we sat there, a pig came familiarly to the door, thrust in his snout, and seemed surprised that he should be driven away, instead of being admitted as one of the family. The floor was of brick; there was no ceiling, but only the peaked gable overhead. The room was kitchen, parlour, and, I suppose, bedroom for the whole family; at all events, there was only the tattered curtain between us and the sleeping accommodations. The good woman either could not or would not speak a word of English, only laughing when S. said, 'Dim Sassenach! 'but she was kind and hospitable, and found a chair for each of us. She had been making some bread, and the dough was on the dresser. Life with these people is reduced to its simplest elements. It is only a pity that they cannot or do not choose to keep themselves cleaner. Poverty, except in cities, need not be squalid. When the shower abated a little, we gave all the pennies we had to the children, and set forth again. By-the-bye, there were several coloured prints stuck up against the walls, and there was a clock ticking in a corner, and some paper-hangings pinned upon the slanting roof.

from *Passages from the English Notebooks* (1870)

A Dull Watering-Place
Rhoda Broughton

Of the few people who know Pen Dyllas, most have an ill word for that small, dull, North Wales watering-place. Innocent of band it is. Neither parade nor pier can it show, and its one pleasure-boat is generally looked upon with a suspicious eye as being liable to the imputation of unseaworthiness. It seems to me to be like a modest young person totally eclipsed, annihilated by its exceedingly full-blown elder sister ugly Ryvel — all lodging-houses and dust and glare. Poor little place! It is only a child of two years old, and not a well grown, well-thriven child either.

Grand days, as to weather, come to despised Pen Dyllas as well as to finer places, and one had come on the 16th of June, 186-. The sun blazed away in his rare glory — rare in these rainy isles — and held out unconcealed threats of sunstroke to any who ventured too impudently into his kingly presence. But in his very fierceness there was benevolence, and nobody was afraid of him. Every ray of light which turned the shabby lodging-house carpets into cloth of gold, every mignonette-sweetened little breeze which stirred the scanty lodging-house curtains, said as plain as could be, 'Come out, come out, and be happy.' The birds said the same; at least they turned it into an anthem, and sang it with a full choir. But it certainly was meltingly hot. The woody hills behind quiet Aber Fynach town were so drowsy that now, at mid-day, they were sleeping soundly, hazy, purple-hollowed, and the road trailed itself along like a dusty white snake.

The same course of reasoning brought everybody to the same conclusion. 'It is too bakingly hot for a long walk. Let us go on the shore.' And so on the shore, towards half past twelve o'clock, you might have seen all the *élite* of Pen Dyllas drinking in the faint ocean wind, thirstily, thriftily, as if afraid of wasting any, and saying in their hearts that God was good. There young men threw stones by thousands and never hit anything, did not intend to, they would have averred, if you had asked them. There muslin-clad damsels paddled daintily with their fingers in little sea-pools and miniature lagoons, and fished out infinitesimal bits of seaweed, and small green crabs, actively unwilling, or filled little fancy baskets with ugly, worthless, dingy stone, changed in the crucible of the imagination into agates, and onyxes, and amethysts. There old people tottered, and basked, and the great sun-god warmed even their froggy old blood for a bit. And the looked out rheumy eyed, over the sea, and pondered, perhaps, on its everlastingness — in its perpetual change, defying change — in contrast to their own short tether. Pondered much, more probably, on their gout, and their port wine, and their knitting, and their grandchildren. And those grandchildren dug, and squabbled, and got coated with dirt, and bored their adoring relatives, after the manner of such small deer.

Not Wisely But Too Well (1867)

Kilvert at Llangollen

Francis Kilvert

Friday, 16th June 1871

At 6 o'clock we left Chester for Llangollen. We walked up through the town to the Hand Hotel, stopping a moment on the fine quaint old grey stone bridge of Dee with its sharp angled recesses, to look down into the clear rocky swift winding river, so like the Wye. As we came near the Hand we heard the strains of a Welsh harp, the first I ever heard. The harper was playing in the hall the air 'Jenny Jones'. I would have come all the way to Llangollen on purpose to hear the Welsh harp. This is the only hotel in Wales where a Welsh harper can be heard. I stood by him entranced while he played 'Llwyn-on' and

'The Roaring of the Valley', and several of the other guests in the house gathered round the harp in the corner of the hall. The harper was a cripple and his crutch rested by his side against a chair. He was a beautiful performer and he was playing on handsome harp of sycamore and ash, which he had won as a prize at an Eisteddfod. I had a good deal of talk with him after he had done playing He told me there were very few people now who could play the Welsh harp and the instrument was fast going out of use. The young people learn the English harp which is much easier being double stringed instead of treble stringed. The Welsh harp has no silver string and it is played from the left shoulder while the English harp is played from the right shoulder. Sir Watkin keeps no harper. His sister does, and her harper is the brother of old Pugh of Dolgelly who took me up Cader Idris. The Llangollen harper said he knew him and thought him a good harper, but his brother whom he also knew and who is dead was much better, the first harper in Wales.

Presently the harper covered his harp and limped away to his own house in the town, saying he should come and play again at 9 o'clock. He plays in the hall at several stated hours every day. He gets nothing from the Hotel and subsists entirely on what visitors give him. At 9 o'clock he came again and played while we were at supper. It was a great and strange delight to listen to the music of the Welsh harp. The house was full of the melody of the beautiful Welsh airs. No wonder when the evil spirit was upon Saul and when David played upon the harp, that Saul was refreshed and was well and that the evil spirit departed from him.

from *Diary*, 1871

Scott Visits the Ladies
James Gibson Lockhart

We proceeded up the hill and found everything about them and their habitation odd and extravagant beyond report. Imagine two women — one apparently seventy and the other sixty-five — dressed in heavy blue riding habits, enormous shoes, and men's hats, with their petticoats so tucked up that at first glance of them, fussing and tottering along their porch in the agony of expectation, we took them for a couple of hazy or crazy old sailors. On nearer inspection they both wear a world of broaches, rings, etc., and Lady Eleanor positively *orders* — several stars and crosses, and a red ribbon, exactly like a K.C.B. To crown all, they have cropt heads, shaggy, rough, bushy, and as white as snow, the one with age alone, the other assisted by a sprinkling of powder. The elder lady is almost blind, and every way much decayed; the other in good preservation. But who could paint the prints, the dogs, the cats, the miniatures, the cram of cabinets, clocks, glass cases, books, bijoterie, dragon china, nodding mandarins, and whirlgigs of every shape and hue — the whole house, outside and in (for we must see everything, to the dressing closets) *covered* with carved oak, very rich and fine some of it; and the illustrated copies of Sir Walter's poems, and the joking, simpering compliments about Waverley and the anxiety to know who McIvor really was, and the absolute devouring of the poor Unknown, who had to carry off, besides all the rest, one small bit of literal *butter* dug up in a Milesian stone jar lately from the bottom of some Irish bog. Great romance (i.e., absurd innocence of character) one must have looked for; but it was confounding to find this mixed up with such eager curiosity and enormous knowledge of the tattle and scandal of the world they had so long left. Their tables were piled high with newspapers from every corner of the kingdom, and they seemed to have the deaths and marriages of the antipodes at their fingers' ends. Their albums and autographs, from Louis XVIII and George IV, down to magazine poets and quack doctors, are a museum. I shall never see the spirit of blue stockingism again in such perfect incarceration. Peveril (a family name for Sir Walter) won't get over their final kissing match for a week. Yet it is too bad to laugh at these good old girls; they have long been the guardian angels of the village, and are worshipped by every man, woman, and child about them.

from Life of Walter Scott (1837)

Thomas Gee

J. Vyrnwy Morgan

Thomas Gee was born in the year of Waterloo. His father had come to Wales at the invitation of Thomas Jones of Denbigh, one of the greatest of Welsh non-conformist leaders to manage a printing press which he had set down for the purpose of producing religious literature in Welsh. Gee, like Saunderson who went to Bala in response to a like invitation from Thomas Charles, was an Englishman; but he domiciled himself in Wales, learnt its language, took to wife one of its daughters; and ultimately, having bought for himself Thomas Jones' printing press, he laid the foundation of the great printing-house at Denbigh, which has been regarded, not without justice, as one of the first of Welsh national assets. Young Thomas Gee was sent to school at Denbigh and Wrexham, returning to Denbigh in 1829, a lad of fourteen, to learn his father's business in the mornings, and to attend school in the afternoons. That he gave obvious promise of his future capacity is clear from the fact that certain astute ecclesiastics sought to entice him into the ministry of the English Church. Had they succeeded, how differently might the history of Wales have had to be written. Fortunately for Wales, he stuck to his trade; and when he was twenty one years of age he was sent up to London to finish his business education, and (though it was no part of the original design) to gain those political ideals his advocacy of which was in time to make his name a household word in the cottages of Wales.

For, in very truth, there was no part of the United Kingdom which stood in need of political enlightenment and leadership as did Wales at that period. Since the Methodist Revival, Welsh interests had been almost exclusively religious. The great non-conformist leaders such as John Elias supported the old political order, though it is interesting to record the fact (which has probably more bearing on our present study than we can together appreciate) that Thomas Jones was altogether radical in his political sympathies. Literature had not been altogether neglected, but it was not a national interest in any very broad sense. Social conditions of the very worst kind had been endured patiently; and there does not seem to have been any very quick or general sense of their injustice or their remediability, or any organised movement for their removal or reform.

Reference has already been made to Thomas Gee's sensitiveness of spirit. He had all the sensitiveness and imagination of the Celt; and this combined with a Teutonic gift of deliberate judgement, gave him the first essential quality of leadership, — the capacity for a true, broad and swift apprehension of the inner meaning of a given situation. When he returned to Wales, it was with this natural gift of leadership quickened by contact with the outer world, with a high passion for political liberty, and its inevitable corollary, religious equality, and with that ideal of nationality which he made it peculiarly his business to establish in Wales. He came back laden with the equipment necessary for the great part which he was in the coming years to play in the life of Wales.

Gee's London life was productive of a friendship which was in the fullness of time to mean much for Wales. The future Sir Hugh Owen had come to London at the same time as Gee; and it is not fanciful to trace to this early friendship that long association of after years which contributed in so great measure to the establishment of the modern Welsh Educational System. It is significant at least that Gee's first definite appearance in the arena of politics was upon the question of education, the occasion being the hostility aroused by Sir James Graham's Education Bill of 1846. In the protest of the following year against the report of the Parliamentary Committee on Welsh Education, a report the character of which is sufficiently indicated by the fact that its appearance has been handed down in Welsh history as *Brad y Llyfrau Gleision*, the 'Blue-Book Betrayal,' Thomas Gee took no small part.

from *Welsh Political and Educational leaders of the Victorian Era* (1908)

The Ecclesiastical Tour
Ronnie Knox-Mawer

Gresford church was not far away. Here we were greeted by the sound of the famous peal. 'The chimes are noted for their sweetness,' the Master Bellringer lectured his attentive audience. Father had come prepared. He opened a small packet from his waistcoat pocket and brought out a pair of Dr Collis Brown's Improved Earplugs.

'Guaranteed to keep out disturbing sound,' he explained.

The Master Bellringer was preparing to take the party up the bell tower. There was no question of Father accompanying them, and I was told that I might not go either. 'You can go completely mad in a bell tower,' Father said. I was very impressed. Perhaps Mr Rathwell would emerge looking like the picture I had seen outside the Hippodrome Cinema of the Hunchback of Notre Dame. The coach party remained up in the bell tower for a surprising length of time, in view of the risks I thought they were taking.

'At least they won't have time now to bother with St Winifred's Well,' Father said to Mother as we waited in the charabanc. He was mistaken. All too soon, we were chugging along the road to Holywell. I ventured to ask father what was this well.

'It's nothing but a hotbed of Romish superstition,' he replied. 'Certainly not worth getting out for,' he told the company at large. He was outvoted. The next moment we were all crowded into the sixteenth-century chapel that overlooked the famous pool. Upon the vaulted walls, various pilgrims had scratched the details of their visit.

'November 12th 1789' read one inscription 'miraculously cured of ye goute. Thanks be to Sainte Winifred.' Someone rashly tried a joke at Father's expense.

'Good job she didn't set up a chemist shop in the High Street, Brother Knox.'

Father was not amused. Under the cloud of his disapproval we returned to our starting point in Wrexham..

Here Father spent some time pointing out how badly the stone of Wrexham Steeple had weathered over the centuries. But this was not his only carp.

'It's no good,' he said to Mrs Rathwell, 'no good at all!'

'How do you mean?' she asked.

Father pointed to the gilded clock-face in the steeple. It had not occurred to the medieval craftsman that this masterpiece would one day be masked by the roof of the Midland Bank and so not visible to Father in the shop.

The following year, Father came forward with a new suggestion. 'As a venue,' he said 'nothing, simply nothing could be more worthwhile than a tour of the chemical works at Cefn.'

The sinister chimneys of the works had been letting out noxious fumes for a hundred years, and employees forced to live in the vicinity were an object of local sympathy.

'They make enough sulphuric acid there to supply not only home but foreign markets as well,' Father urged. 'And in the very latest of laboratories.'

'Perhaps another time, Brother,' soothed Mr Rathwell.

'Never put off to the morrow what can be arranged today,' came the reply.

It was to no avail. His suggestion was turned down.

'Then I shall go myself,' he declared. 'And that boy can come along with me,' he added, as an afterthought.

For once Mother spoke out.

'Not with his chest, dear,' she said.

On his return, Father dubbed the works the Eighth Wonder of Wales. 'Worth all the rest of them put together.'

The Welsh Tourist Board has yet to agree with Father's view. But then his was usually a minority opinion; ahead of his time, maybe.

from *Tales of a Man Called Father* (1989)

Henry M. Stanley
Askew Roberts

. . . if any of our tourist friends are of an enquiring turn of mind, and have leisure on their hands, they may attempt to discover the parentage of the discoverer of Livingstone, who, as 'Henry M. Stanley' repudiates the youth 'John Rowlands,' the native of Denbigh some Welshmen say he is.

from *The Gossiping Guide to Wales* (1881)

Hiraeth
John Lloyd

Talking about going to America and actually going are two different things. Many of my friends came to see me off down the river. They looked worriedly at me and I at them. It was a shaky first step from the landing stage onto the ship. As we sailed those who were left behind waved their handkerchiefs, their hands and their hats above their heads. Oh! oh! there was Liverpool disappearing from our sight Soon we could see the shores of Flintshire, and when opposite Rhyl, ah! there was the dear Clwyd Valley as if opening before me and a feeling of *hiraeth* came over me when I remembered that Pont'ralltgoch lay in that direction and as I caught sight of the haunts of my youth I shed a tear.

Letter from New York to his parents in Pont'ralltgoch near
St Asaph, August 1868.

Edward Lloyd and Perpetual Motion
Wynford Vaughan Thomas

We had been so long in the lonely places, riding over moorlands and through unfrequented lanes that we had forgotten that there was such a thing as the motor-car or that the main roads of Britain have become race tracks. This road up the valley of the Dee carries most of the holiday traffic towards Snowdonia in the summer. Riding along it was like riding on the back of a circular saw — every car that passed gave an angry protesting snarl at seeing the outmoded horse usurping the place needed by the internal-combustion engine. We covered about half a mile of this petrol-soaked race-track that calls itself A5, the successor of the great highway that Telford built to speed up the Irish mail in the old coaching days. Then we turned gratefully down to cross the Dee and join the quiet, winding road that runs on the other side of the valley. We watered the horses in the Dee.

'Bit better than the other road,' a friendly farmer said to us as he saw us bring the horses back out of the water. 'I never go over the other side till September.' 'Talk about perpetual motion,' I said; 'that traffic's the nearest to it I ever saw.' 'Well, a funny thing you should talk of perpetual motion, because they say that it was along that very stretch of road that Edward Lloyd drove his machine. And some still say that he had found the secret.' There and then, he told me the strange story of the nineteenth-century engineer, Edward Lloyd, who is buried in the churchyard at Glyndyfrdwy. Apparently this gifted and eccentric man made a great impression on the valley in the days when few people penetrated its quiet seclusion. He worked in secret. No one knew quite what he was up to until one morning, the inhabitants were astonished to see a large drum-like object bowling gently along the road. 'My grandather always used to say that he saw it himself. There was no doubt about it. The wheel went on and on and there was nothing to show what was driving the thing along. Of course, nothing came of it because Edward Lloyd wanted to keep the secret to himself — died with him, I think.'

I wonder. I'm no mathematician and the whole business of perpetual motion may be mathematically impossible, but perhaps Edward Lloyd had found some secret that had eluded more orthodox-minded men.

from *Madly in All Directions* (1967)

The One-legged Fisherman
Washington Irving

In a morning stroll along the banks of the Alyn, a beautiful little stream which flows down from the Welsh hills and throws itself into the Dee, my attention was attracted to a group seated on the margin. On approaching I found it to consist of a veteran angler and two rustic disciples. The former was an old fellow, with a wooden leg, with clothes very well but very carefully patched, betokening poverty, honestly come by, and decently maintained. His face bore the marks of former storms, but present fair weather; its furrows had been worn into a habitual smile; his iron-grey locks hung about his ears, and he had altogether the good humoured air of a constitutional philosopher who was disposed to take the world as it went....

The old man was busy in examining the maw of a trout which he had just killed, to discover by the contents which insects were seasonable for bait; and was lecturing to his companions, who appeared to listen with infinite deference.

I could not but remark the gallant manner in which the veteran angler stumped from one part of the brook to another; waving his rod in the air, to keep the line from dragging on the ground, or catching among the bushes; and the adroitness with which he would throw his fly to any particular place; sometimes swimming it along a little rapid; sometimes casting it into one of those dark holes made by a twisted root or overhanging bank in which the large trout are apt to lurk. In the meantime he was giving instructions to his two disciples: showing them the manner in which they should handle their rods, fix their flies, and play them along the surface of the stream.

It was part of the great plain of Cheshire, close by the beautiful vale of Gresford, and just where the inferior Welsh hills begin to swell up from fresh-smelling meadows. The day, too, like that recorded in Walton's great work, was mild and sunshiny, with now and then a soft-dropping shower that sowed the whole earth with diamonds.

I fell into conversation with the old angler and was so much entertained that, under pretext of receiving instructions in his art, I kept company with him almost the whole day; wandering along the banks of the stream, and listening to his talk. He was very communicative, having all the easy garrulity of cheerful old age; and I fancy was a little flattered by having an opportunity of displaying his piscatorial lore;

for who does not like now and then to play the sage?

He had been much of a rambler in his day, and had passed some years of his youth in America, particularly in Savannah, where he had entered into trade, and had been ruined by the indiscretion of a partner. He had afterwards experienced many ups and downs in life, until he got into the navy, where his leg was carried away by a cannon ball at the Battle of Camperdown.

This was the only stroke of real good fortune he had ever experienced, for it got him a pension which together with some small paternal property brought him in a revenue of nearly forty pounds. On this he retired to his native village, where he lived quietly and independently, and devoted the remainder of his life to 'the noble art of angling'.

I found that he had read Izaak Walton attentively, and he seemed to have imbibed all his simple frankness and prevalent good humour.

On parting with the old angler I inquired after his place of abode, and, happening to be in the neighbourhood of the village a few days afterwards, I had the curiosity to seek him out. I found him living in an old cottage, containing only one room, but a perfect curiosity in its method and arrangement. It was on the skirts of the village, on a green bank, a little back from the road, with a small garden in front, stocked with kitchen herbs and adorned with a few flowers. The whole front of the cottage was overrun with a honeysuckle. On the top was a ship for a weathercock. The interior was filled up in a truly nautical style, his ideas of comfort and convenience having been acquired on the berth-deck of a man-of-war . . . . His implements for angling were carefully disposed on nails and hooks about the room. On a shelf was arranged his library, containing a work on angling, much worn, a Bible covered with canvas, an old volume or two of voyages, a nautical almanack and a book of songs.

I found him seated on a bench before the door smoking his pipe in the soft evening sunshine. His cat was purring soberly on the threshold, and his parrot describing some strange evolutions in an iron ring, that swung in the centre of his cage. He had been angling all day, and gave me a history of his sport with as much minuteness as a general would talk over a campaign, being particularly animated in relating the manner in which he had taken a large trout, which had completely tasked all his skill and wariness, and which he had sent as a trophy to mine hostess of the inn.

The whole tenor of his life was quiet and inoffensive, being principally passed about the neighbouring streams, when the weather and season were favourable; and at other times he employed himself at home, preparing his fishing tackle for the next campaign, or manufacturing rods, nets, and floes for his patrons and pupils among the gentry.

from *The Sketch Book* (1820)

The Ill-fated Launch
Nathaniel Hawthorne

August 2nd,1855
Mr. — has urged me very much to go with his father and family to see the launch of a great ship which has been built for their house, and afterwards to partake of a picnic; so, on Tuesday morning I presented myself at the landing-stage, and met the party, to take passage for Chester. It was a showery morning, and looked woefully like a rainy day; but nothing better is to be expected in England; and, after all, there is seldom such a day that you cannot glide about pretty securely between the drops of rain. This, however, did not turn out one of those tolerable days, but grew darker and darker, and worse and worse; and was worst of all when we had passed about six miles beyond Chester, and were just on the borders of Wales, on the hither side of the river Dee, where the ship was to be launched. Here the train stopped, and absolutely deposited our whole party of excursionists, under a heavy shower, in the midst of a muddy potato-field, whence we were to wade through mud and mire to the ship-yard, almost half a mile off. Some kind Christian, I know not whom, gave me half of his umbrella, and half of his cloak, and thereby I got to a shed near the ship, without being entirely soaked through.

The ship had been built on the banks of the Dee, at a spot where it is too narrow for her to be launched directly across, and so she lay lengthwise of the river, and was so arranged as to take water parallel with the stream. She is, for aught I know, the largest ship in the world; at any rate, longer than the Great Britain, — an iron-screw steamer, — and looked immense and magnificent, and was gorgeously dressed out in flags. Had it been a pleasant day, all Chester and half Wales would have been there to see the launch; and, in spite of the rain, there were a good many people on the opposite shore, as well as on our side; and one or two booths, and many of the characteristics of a fair, — that is to say, men and women getting intoxicated without any great noise and confusion.

The ship was expected to go off at about twelve o'clock, and at that juncture all Mr. —'s friends assembled under the bows of the ship, where we were little sheltered from the rain by the projection of that part of the vessel over our heads. The bottle of port wine with which she was to be christened was suspended from the bows to the platform where we stood by a blue ribbon; and the ceremony was to be performed by Mrs. —, who, I could see, was very nervous in anticipation of the ceremony. Mr. — kept giving her instructions in a whisper, and showing her how to throw the bottle, and as the critical moment approached, he took hold of it along with her. All this time we were waiting in momentary expectation of the ship going off, everything being ready, and only the touch of a spring, as it were, needed to make her slide into the water. But the chief manager kept delaying a little longer, and a little longer; though the pilot on board sent to tell him that it was time she was off. 'Yes, yes; but I want as much water as I can get,' answered the manager; and so he held on till, I suppose, the tide had raised the river Dee to its very acme of height. At last the word was given; the ship began slowly to move; Mrs.— threw the bottle against the bow with a spasmodic effort that dashed it into a thousand pieces, and diffused the fragrance of the old port all around, where it lingered several minutes. I did not think that there could have been such a breathless moment in an affair of this kind.

The ship moved majestically down toward the river; and unless it were Niagara, I never saw anything grander and more impressive than the motion of this mighty mass as she departed from us. We on the platform, and everybody along both shores of the Dee, took off our hats in the rain, waved handkerchiefs, cheered, shouted,— 'Beautiful!' 'What a noble launch!' 'Never was so fair a sight!' — and, really, it was so grand, that calm, majestic movement, that I felt the tears come into my eyes. The wooden pathway adown which she was gliding began to smoke with the friction; when all at once, when we expected to see her plunge into the Dee, she came to a full stop. Mr.—, the father of my friend, a gentleman with white hair, a dark, expressive face, bright eyes, and an Oriental cast of features, immediately took the alarm. A moment before his countenance had been kindled with triumph; but now he turned pale as death, and seemed to grow ten years older while I was looking at him. Well he might, for his noble ship was stuck fast in the mud of the Dee, and without deepening the bed of the river, I do not see how her vast iron hulk is ever to be got out.

from *Passages from the English Notebooks* (1870)

Mr Phillips
Daniel Owen

Although St. Mary's Church where Gwen Tomos worshipped occasionally on Sunday evenings was but an ordinary structure compared with modern churches, even in rural areas, she was surprised, as soon as she entered Tan-y-fron Chapel, at its dull austere appearance and at the complete absence of nearly everything likely to add to the comfort of the congregation. Every seat in the chapel was occupied and there were many people standing. Gwen's presence at the service caused considerable surprise, and a dozen or more people offered their seats to her and Elin. She was embarrassed to find herself the centre of attention, but she realised that it was only to be expected as she was a stranger there, and futhermore, she was the only one dressed in her Sunday best. Most of the congregation were in their working clothes, and even Elin had not changed from the dress which she wore for the market that afternoon. Gwen had always gone to church in her best clothes, and indeed she could claim that even the parson's daughter had never been better attired. She felt some shame that she should be so elegantly dressed, and she would have been even more so had she realised that Elin's father, Robert Owen, the deacon, was praying and beseeching God to touch the heart of the 'proud hussy'. Fortunately for her, she had no idea that Robert Owen was referring to her.

After the prayer, the door near the pulpit opened, and everyone's eyes turned in that direction to see Mr. Phillips coming in. Everyone knows the effect on a large crowd of the arrival of a long awaited speaker. In some circumstances, the audience shows its feeling by cheering loudly, but as this cannot be done in a place of worship, the relief of the congregation could be seen in the happy expression on the faces of everyone. They all forgot about Gwen Tomos as they gazed upon the eloquent preacher, and she herself was confirmed in her belief that she had never before seen such a handsome man. She forgot the austere appearance of the chapel as everything seemed transformed by Mr. Phillips's presence. In a melodious voice, with an accent less broad than is usually heard in the north and one that suited him well, he read the first hymn which the congregation sang, from memory, with great fervour. Gwen felt herself being lifted into a feeling of ecstasy, but she could not shake off the consciousness of guilt for being there. The preacher then read the parable of the ten virgins, and followed it with a prayer full of warmth and emotion. Gwen had not heard a spontaneous prayer before, and she had never imagined it possible to pray without the aid of a prayer book. For his text, Mr. Phillips took the parable of the barren fig tree and when he described the vineyards of the east, the vine and the fig tree, and began developing his theme, she was carried away by his words. Suddenly she took fright and feared that she might be converted to Methodism, and she made up her mind not to listen to the preacher and to think of other things. She looked around and saw that everyone was listening intently and trying to follow the sermon. She felt ashamed at being different from everyone else and once again turned her mind and her thoughts to the preacher. She tried to think of him rather than what he was saying, but she soon realised that Elin was right when she said that Mr. Phillips would soon be forgotten in his sermon. Having tried every device to escape his message, Gwen had eventually to listen to him and she was carried away by his fervour and eloquence. Mr. Phillips described the qualities of various sinners, now and again asking, 'What sayeth the husbandman of this? Cut it down!' One can well imagine the impact of such oratory on a sensitive girl like Gwen, accustomed only to the monotonous intonation of the old parish parson.

from *Gwen Tomos* (1894) trans. T. Ceiriog Williams & E.R. Harries

A Pothersome Pair
John Ceiriog Hughes

Once a sleepy wife there was
    In Llan Mathafarn dwelling:
Would not for her husband wake
    Though he was hoarse with yelling.

'Heigh ho,' she spake, laid like a pancake,
And he cried in his sorrow,
'If you're not ill, rise with a will
Or lie there till tomorrow.'

Ten o'clock, and kids let out
A blaring row that second:
When she'd calmed them with a shout,
Said she but half-awakened,
'Illness or such, you don't know much!'
But he said, 'Damn your scorning!
Yawning's the taint of your complaint
And has been every morning!'

But the husband, all too soon,
Contracted his wife's ailment:
Now the household sleeps till noon
And all without curtailment.
Gander nor goose flies down from roost,
Make breakfast or fire kindle,
And on my life, husband and wife
In equal slumber mingle.

trans. Tony Conran

A Poet's Juvenalia

Wilfred Owen

Aug. 16. 1905

Dear Mother

I am so sorry you were not well on Sunday. I thought about you very often, nearly all day. We climbed Moel Famma (Varma) on the 14th. I was rather exhausted by the time we reached the top. It was about 4 o'clock, started at 11.30, but when we got home I was hardly so bad as the others were. Alec made a show of sliding down the smooth slippery grass but he found he could not stop himself. He went bounding on till he was suddenly checked by a sharp stone wall. We thought he had hurt his head but he had a deep cut on the knee, he said he was able to climb the hill though! I was lying down at the time resting. Thank you very much for the letter & Turkish Delight. I have had a little bad luck. Up Moel Famma I lost my big fat knife I think. I am very sorry to say I broke the end of your umbrella. We tried to fish with the end of our rods in a tiny stream that runs into the Clwyd. I lent Alec a hook which he lost, & I lost my own, & cracked the tip end of my rod. I have bought a Picture Postcard for Harold which I hope to send tomorrow.

With best love to all,
From
Wilfred.

from *Journey from Obscurity*, ed. Harold Owen (1963)

Three Hinds of Denbighshire

Anon.

My day, my news, my night, my mind,
my forgiveness, you're near me
and I am waiting meekly:
even if you'll be my enemy, come.

All joy, all empty jollity, all thought,
every mannerly companion,
everything indeed but longing
has suddenly gone away from me.

There's a river, a hillside and fresh boughs of trees
that hide three hinds:
today no hunter finds
them or tries their willing flesh.

The morning you'll be ready, concerned
with deer hunting:
not one prey are we proposing
but a notable group of three.

Not with dogs should you decide to hunt us —
that wouldn't be luckiest;
better for you, my love, to tryst
under trees with your dogs tied.

trans. Gwyn Williams

Old Hughes of Kinmel
George Cornwallis West

We were given permission by old Mr. Hughes, of Kinmel — a name to conjure with in North Wales in those days — to fish the Elwy, a sporting little stream which runs into the Clwyd below St. Asaph. 'Old Hughes of Kinmel', as he was always called, one of the most noble characters of his day, lived to a great age, and almost to the day of his death his hair and beard remained a beautiful black, though my father uncharitably declared that towards the end of every fortnight they were bottle green! Being a typical Victorian the only two forms of headgear he ever wore were a tall silk hat or an even taller one of ordinary felt. He usually affected a blue coat edged with broad mohair braid and tight sponge-bag trousers, and was the last man I knew who wore a fob instead of a watch-chain.

One day when we were fishing the Kinmel water old Mr. Hughes happened to come along the river, and we all three went up and thanked him for his kindness in giving us permission to fish there. With true Victorian courtesy he asked us whether we had had any sport, and when we answered in the affirmative suggested that he might have a look in our fishing baskets. As we were having a competition and consequently everything counted, to our shame it must be admitted that we had failed to return to the water many young salmon smolts which we had caught, and it was in fear and trembling that we offered up our catch for inspection. In a stern voice he demanded to know whether we were aware of the penalties which might be inflicted for the non-return of young salmon to the river. Mowbray acted as spokesman and explained the exigencies of the occasion.

'It's just as well for you,' said the old gentleman, 'that I and not the river keeper have found you out.' He then proceeded to ask for a solemn promise from all three of us that this 'disgraceful piece of poaching' should not be repeated, otherwise leave to fish would be withdrawn. When he had exacted the promise, he pointed out that it would be as well if he took possession of the smolts in case the keeper came along. 'I do not wish to rob you of your catch,' he explained, 'I propose to purchase them,' and he gave us each half a crown and wound up with an invitation to tea that evening!

from *Edwardians Go Fishing* (1932)

An Urban Impact
Emlyn Williams

It was my first train journey; the week-end bustle of the tiny station, the parcels, the porters, the smell of the sea and then, out of nowhere, the ruthlessly steady approach of the monster, the smoke and the whistle-shrieks and the door-bangs, it all excited and frightened me. Mam sat like a statue, a bundle on each side — I never saw her trust anything to a luggage-rack-and her eyes fixed on the communication cord as we shot past a vast black, smoking, crashing, burning, devilish city which she said was the Mostyn Ironworks. The estuary to the left, and several stops; but nothing so good happened again till Shotton, where Dad awaited us, straight from work, washed and brushed and smiling, proud of us and himself.

I clutched at my parents with my eyes — my hands were full of luggage — and thought, I must not lose sight of them, I shall be swallowed up in this eddy of faces and voices and houses and shops and footsteps, I cannot take it in, I cannot . . . . Shotton and Connah's Quay, merging into each other with indifference on both sides, were at that time a couple of hasty townships, wood and bricks and mortar run up at the behest of commerce; but on me, that busy Saturday, they had the effect of strong drink. Not only were the bicycles going quicker and ringing sharper bells, but the people with the preoccupied faces were walking brisker, the smoke from the strange houses blew faster, and even the town-clouds, brown at the edges from smuts and sophistication, raced swifter over a man-made sky. My head swam with the multiplication of fellow-beings, with the plurality of shops (ten in a row!) and with the danger of being lost. The swarthy old woman with the limp and the hat with a feather, swaying round a corner — had she gone for ever? Had I seen her? There was a man playing a cornet, for pennies, with a cap at his crippled feet, a man dedicated to sadness — I must have had a small fever, that Saturday-he was the beggar outside the Opera House to whom Mifanwy slips a sovereign, the maimed slave in the dust of the Colosseum, he was Life, half of it the life which was undoubtedly his, squatting there, and half the life which I breathed, the breath of fiction . . . .

from *George* (1961)

Commemoration
T.E. Ellis

I think nothing is more attractive in the villages where they still survive than the old Celtic crosses of the early centuries. They are silent witnesses to the generations that have passed away in those villages, and they are witnesses to this day of the beauty of the design and of the instinctive skill which a Welshman in the early, the 9th, 10th, and 11th centuries possessed. I shall be extremely glad when villagers themselves, or those who have left villages and prospered in the world and go back again, realise what a service they do to a village if they help to raise, not perhaps a village cross, but some form of village monument to those who either in the village or out of it have done credit to their birth- place and service to humanity.

I was one day last summer in an out-of-the-way little village, called Llansannan, which is considered to be a completely out-of-the-world place. There you find at the present day some of the most characteristic Welshmen of the whole of Wales. There you find certain freshness and vigour of spirit and of activity and a great deal of splendid conservatism on the part of the villagers and the peasants, and I felt as I looked upon the open square of the little village that it would be a real addition to that village and something that would, perhaps, kindle the young mind there, if a fitting monument, say a Celtic cross, such as you find in Pembrokeshire and in many parts of Ireland, were raised in honour of the men who have been reared in that parish. Four names at once occur to me as being worthy to be placed side by side or one after another on such a village cross. For a parish which has produced at various ages Tudur Aled, William Salisbury, William Rees, and Henry Rees, is a parish which can be very proud of itself, and a parish which ought, I think, to rear for generations of its children a monument to show that it appreciates the services which men who have been reared and who have lived in that parish have rendered not only to that countryside but to the whole of Wales, and some of them to humanity.

from *Speeches and Addresses* (1912)

The Privilege
T. Gwynn Jones

Now he was dumb,
on his bed at his last hour,
after long and diligent life,
calm when light and when dark alike,
his path straight along its length;
from acre to acre it was worthy.

His last evening's rest was nearing,
the dumb departure
from the fair familiar place of his ancestors,
dearest place that he would see no more.

These from day to day he had been wise,
gentle and courteous;
a man of judgement and strength,
generous with his favours;
his care was a beacon amid the world's changes,
as he knew that scholarship which gives life to the wise —
that which will, from now on, be too simple and old in its morality
to us in our proud lack of understanding —
a part of the gentility of Edeirnion,
of the integrity of its races and its civilised nature,
now was parting from it;
after this there would no longer be found there
either his cultured speech or his genial smile.

People

And from now on he was dumb . . .
the words of the old language he loved,
that had been a long age on his lips,
would not come tonight.

On a book that was there by his bed,
he slowly turned his gaze,
and the one who watched him saw
his dumb desire.

And he reached the book from its shelf,
and held it up and turned its ancient pages,
one by one with a gentle hand;
and for that much of a poor favour,
however profitless it was on this last threshold,
his two eyes lit up again just once,
a moment of the old light . . .

And his face shone still as he watched
the pages there being turned, until his eyes fell
upon some words which would alone, now,
give speech to his last hour . . .

And his finger wandered to the place,
the place he asked for,
and stayed there on the words —
'My bow I placed in the cloud,
and it will be a sign of a covenant
between me and the earth.'

And he retreated into that last mystery . . .
and the Privilege marked his death.

trans. R. Gerallt Jones

A World Beyond

Hugh Evans

The mail coach ran along the turnpike road in summer; but that was no mode of travelling for the people of Cwm Eithin. The mail coach was for 'gentry', and if one of the Cwm Eithin people had been seen outside the coach it would have provided his neighbours with material for a month's gossip. They followed their lawful vocations on horseback, in their traps, in carts or on foot, and they thought nothing of walking to the nearest town, a distance of some ten miles, heavily laden on the journey out and home. They were magnificent walkers. Droves of cattle, horses, pigs, sheep and geese passed along the turnpike on their way from Wales to England, and at some seasons of the year the fields around Cerrig y Drudion would be full of animals resting for the night. It was at Cerrig y Drudion that the cattle were shod, to protect their feet on the long trek on the hard high road . . .

Geese were poor walkers and the goose driver had to be a patient man. I understand that geese were shod for the journey in olden times, the method being to steep their feet in pitch, but that was before my day. I cannot remember that I ever saw a flock of hens passing by; hens were particular and insisted upon being carried. I have heard that Joe of Henblas once tried to take a flock to Ruthin on foot but the attempt was not successful. Perhaps that may have been accounted for by the fact that Joe was a simpleton. One evening his mistress said: 'Joe, we must get the hens ready for Ruthin now; there will be no time in the morning.' Joe went out at once and brought all the hens down from their perches. His intention was to make a drove of them there and then, but the hens had no experience of that sort of thing and scattered all over the place. Joe ran until he was exhausted and then returned, very hot and bothered, to the house. 'Mistress,' said he, 'I can make nothing of those old hens. They run, one *gog gog* that way, and the other *gog gog* the other way!'

You will see, therefore, that although the people of Cwm Eithin lived in a glen, they were not ignorant of the outside world. They knew that one end of the glen opened in the direction of a rich and fertile country called England. They had three facts to prove that such a country existed beyond all doubt:

1. They had seen thousands upon thousands of horses, cattle, sheep, pigs and geese on their way to England, and of all those

thousands not one traveller returned. The drovers came back, saying there was plenty of room for more. It must, the people decided, be a very big country.

2. The cattle dealers who came from England had plenty of money to pay for the cattle they bought. It must be a very rich country.

3. Some of the men of the glen went to Shropshire every year to the wheat harvest, and on their return they would say they had had their fill of wheaten bread. England must be a very fertile country. This made Cwm Eithin people who lived on barley bread wish for a whiter loaf, but not for a happier place to live in.

from *The Gorse Glen* (1931), trans. E. Morgan Humphreys

Philip Yorke, The Last Squire of Erddig
Adam Mars-Jones

A hitch-hiking student extends his thumb doubtfully in front of Philip's car; very little more would be needed to stop it forever. There is a bicycle lying loosely on its roof-rack, like the lifeboat on a liner. All the lights and signals on one side (plus one windscreen-wiper) are out of action; it has had a stroke or something quite similar, but it hasn't bounced back the way Philip did after his. Philip tells him that since it says Morris on the car's bonnet and Austin on the boot, it must be a Mostyn. Wanting only a lift to Llangollen, the student finds himself diverted to a farm, where the two of them feed a pair of half-wild cats, and Philip makes kissing noises over the fence at a flock of unamused sheep. Then Philip leads him to a privy, in which three ancient motor-bikes stand rusting. Philip wheels out a massive Matchless and fiddles with it until his hands are covered with petrol; then he straddles it and asks to be pushed down the path. When the engine roars, Philip shouts at his helper to hop on; then as if two on a bike wasn't a quorum, he shouts at a farm-worker in the distance to join them. Getting no answer, Philip sets off across the bumpy field anyway. After this experience with the bike, the hitch-hiker is relieved when their next stop in the car is only a church. Philip rattles the collection-box, wonders aloud if the Catholics have raided it, and stuffs it with money. There is money everywhere about his person: statements of dividend on stock (in tobacco firms and distilleries mainly, wickedness at second hand), and plenty of cash. Today The Yorke Is *Very* Rich, Philip murmurs; he has notes salted away in different pockets, in wallets and envelopes, loose or tied with rubber bands, like a squirrel with an autumn of foresight and a winter of forgetfulness compressed into each transaction. From church Philip briefly rejoins the route for Llangollen to buy a rum-and-raisin choc-ice, then turns right round to pick up some clean clothes from the launderette at Rhosllanerchrugog. By this time the hitch-hiker is reconciled to rambling strangeness, and makes no more protest than the wasted mongrel in the back seat. The party ends up in a terraced house in Ruabon, where amongst other places Philip is based; the hitch-hiker has to duck as he enters, to avoid low-slung light-bulbs. Philip starts a fire and ignites the chimney, or so a policeman knocking at the front door tells him. He makes coffee with water straight out of the tap and pronounces it wonderful. An elderly man arrives and immediately retires to the front room to sort out Philip's correspondence; Philip is capable of ignoring any number of Stamped Self-Addressed Envelopes, and without Brownie's visits every few months his affairs would simply seize up. Brownie will accept only a cup of hot water, believing everything else in the world to be an irritant, and leaves as soon as the job is done. The hiker is retained to help with the task of making up a double bed with single-size fitted sheets. Then Philip makes supper of instant soup, ice cream, and biscuits, murmuring If It's Wet It's Clean as he pulls plates from a greasy sink. He shows off his most prized possession, a pewter plate-holder he prefers to anything on show to the public at Erddig. He explains that he likes living here better than in the big house, because You Can't Live off a View; and paintings and mirrors are wonderful but they can't stop you from burning your hands. The hitch-hiker spends a miserable night between the nylon sheets he has helped, inadequately, to fix up; but Philip's morning porridge restores him. Philip insists on giving him some money when he goes, but salves wounded pride by calling it a loan; he writes 4 Tai Clawdd Ruabon, the address to which it should be returned, on each banknote.

from *Lantern Lecture* (1981)

The Scholarship Boy
Emlyn Williams

Miss Moffat (*rising and pacing towards the desk*): The villagers are all in their best, and talking about a holiday tomorrow. It is very stupid of them, because if you have failed it will make you still more sick at heart

Morgan: If I have failed? (*In sudden desperation.*) Don't speak about it!

Miss Moffat (*turning to him, surprised*): But we must! You faced the idea the day you left for Oxford.

Morgan: I know, but I have been to Oxford, and come back, since then! (*Sitting on the lower end of the sofa, facing her.*) I have come back — from the world! Since the day I was born, I have been a prisoner behind a stone wall, and now somebody has given me a leg-up to have a look at the other side . . . (*vehement*) . . . they cannot drag me back again, they cannot, they *must* give me a push and send me over!

Miss Moffat (*sitting beside him, half-touched, half-amused*): I've never heard you talk so much since I've known you.

Morgan: That is just it! I *can* talk, now! The three days I have been there, I have been talking my head off!

Miss Moffat: Ha! If three days at Oxford can do that to you, what would you be like at the end of three years?

Morgan: That's just it again — it would be everything I need, everything! Starling and I spent three hours one night discussin' the law — Starling, you know, the brilliant one . . . . The words came pouring out of me — all the words that I had learnt and written down and never spoken — I suppose I was talking nonsense, but I was at least holding a conversation! I suddenly realised that I had never done it before — I had never been *able* to do it. (*With a strong Welsh accent.*) 'How are you, Morgan? Nice day, Mr Jones! Not bad for the harvest!' — a vocabulary of twenty words; all the thoughts that you have given to me were being stored away as if they were always going to be useless — locked up and rotting away — a lot of questions with nobody to answer them, a lot of statements with nobody to contradict them ... and there I was with Starling, nineteen to the dozen. (*Suddenly quieter.*) I came out of his rooms that night, and I walked down the High. That's their High Street, you know.

Miss Moffat (*nodding, drinking in the torrent with the most intense pleasure*): Yes, yes . . .

Morgan (looking before him): I looked up, and there was a moon behind Magd — Maudlin. Not the same moon I have seen over the Nant, a different face altogether. Everybody seemed to be walking very fast, with their gowns on, in the moonlight; the bells were ringing, and I was walking faster than anybody and I felt — well, the same as on the rum in the old days!
Miss Moffat: Go on.
Morgan: All of a sudden, with one big rush, against that moon, and against that High Street . . . I saw this room; you and me sitting here studying, and all those books — and everything I have ever learnt from those books, and from you, was lighted up — like a magic lantern —ancient Rome, Greece, Shakespeare, Carlyle, Milton . . . everything had a meaning, because I was in a new world — my world! And so it came to me why you worked like a slave to make me ready for his scholarship . . . . (*Lamely.*) I've finished.

from *The Corn is Green* (1935)

Thinking of the Dead
Robert Graves

In November came the Armistice. I heard at the same time of the deaths of Frank Jones-Bateman, who had gone back again just before the end, and Wilfred Owen, who often used to send me poems from France. Armistice-night hysteria did not touch our camp much, though some of the Canadians stationed there went down to Rhyl to celebrate in true overseas style. The news sent me out walking alone along the dyke above the marshes of Rhuddlan (an ancient battlefield, the Flodden of Wales), cursing and sobbing and thinking of the dead.

Siegfried's famous poem celebrating the Armistice began:

Everybody suddenly burst out singing,
And I was filled with such delight
As prisoned birds must find in freedom . . .

But 'everybody' did not include me.

from *Goodbye To All That* (1929)

The Elusive Steak
John Moore

Unless you have seen one, you cannot possibly imagine what a Welsh Sunday is like. It is a day of penance and black wrath, of such gloom and misery that in Wales alone among the nations must men look forward to Monday morning with keen delight. I will try to describe it as I saw it, this Sunday evening at Colwyn Bay.

The sky had clouded over and it was drizzling rather wretchedly. The streets were full of people who had nothing to do and nowhere to go, and who walked with that purposeless slouch which one sees in Limehouse. The public houses were locked and barred of course, and no merry voices came from them; shut also was the cinema and were all the shops. A skeleton bus service was running, but it was quite inadequate, and little groups of people who wanted (presumably) to get away from Colwyn Bay stood about waiting for buses, getting wet. And up and down the streets, hopelessly and purposelessly, tramped a thousand miserable victims of the prohibitionist-complex, of the almost pathological desire to prevent people from enjoying themselves. Holiday-makers who had come from afar in charabancs and so had nowhere to shelter, stood in doorways and looked out at the rain. Small children with solemn faces stood in doorways and looked out at the rain. Lovers whose own houses were cramped and unfriendly to love-making stood in doorways and held hands and looked out at the rain.

My desire for a steak had now crystallised in my mind into an acute need of one. But here was a difficulty: I went to four restaurants, and they were all shut. Surely there must be one open somewhere; surely it was legitimate to eat a steak at Colwyn Bay on Sunday! I went and asked a policeman about it.

'Well,' he said, thinking, 'if you went just round the corner you might get an egg.'

An egg! He might just as well have offered me mother's milk, in the mood I was in. An egg! Had I not eggs enough and to spare in my tent, and was I not sick of eggs, and hungry as a ravening lion? Gently I explained to the policeman that I wanted a steak. 'Ah,' he said 'if you went to dinner at one of the hotels . . .' but he looked a little doubtfully at my shorts as he suggested it, and I knew what he was thinking.

No, I told him, it was not an hotel I wanted; but just a restaurant, a very modest café, where I could obtain, for a sum not exceeding two shillings, a grilled steak, some fried potatoes, and perhaps, with luck, even some chipped onions. Was there no such place, or was it not lawful?

The policeman shook his head sadly. They were all shut. There was nowhere.

By now the steak had assumed monstrous and desirable proportions in my mind. I wanted it above all things; and obstinately, I would be content with nothing else. Eve herself cannot have ached more keenly to taste the Forbidden Fruit . . . .

And so, moved by some wicked spirit, I began to swear. I went on swearing, unrepetitive, in a low monotone. It is never a wise thing to swear before a policeman. He stared at me in astonishment, then he spoke. 'Here,' he said, 'you mustn't do that! If you go on doing that I shall have to take you up, I shall. What are you swearing about like that?'

'I'll tell you,' I said. And very carefully in Welsh now — in fluent but rather unacademic Welsh — I told him. I told him that there was only one place that Colwyn Bay really resembled on Sunday, and that place was *uffern*. Like unto like, said I; *similia similibus curantur*. And so, for its own good, to *uffern* I condemned Colwyn Bay, and the meek uncomplaining inhabitants of Colwyn Bay, and particularly the City Fathers of Colwyn Bay, who would not let me eat a steak on Sunday ...and then I left him, gaping, before he could arrest me.

from *Tramping Through Wales* (1931)

Jones
H.G. Wells

I expected a library, playing fields, a room of my own. I expected fresh air and good plain living. I thought all Wales was lake and mountain and wild loveliness. And the Holt Academy had the added advantage of re-opening at the end of July and so shortening the gap of impecuniosity after the College of Science dispersed. But when I got to Holt I found only the decaying remains of a once prosperous institution set in a dismal street of houses in a flat ungainly landscape. Holt was a small old town shrunk to the dimensions of a village, and its most prominent feature was a gasometer. The school house was an untidy dwelling with what seemed to be a small whitewashed ex-chapel, with broken and dirty windows and a brick floor, by way of schoolroom. The girls' school was perhaps a score of children and growing girls in a cramped little villa down the street. The candidates for the ministry were three lumpish young men apparently just off the fields, and the boys' school was a handful of farmers' and shop-keepers' sons. My new employer presented himself as a barrel of a man with bright eyes in a round, ill-shaven face, a glib tongue and a staccato Welsh accent, dressed in the black coat, white tie and top hat dear to Tommy Morley, the traditional garb of the dominie. He was dirty, — I still remember his blackened teeth — and his wife was dirty, with a certain life-soiled prettiness. He conducted me to a bedroom which I was to share, I learnt, with two of the embryo Calvinistic ministers.

My dismay deepened as I went over the premises and discovered the routines of the place. The few boarders were crowded into a room or so, sleeping two and three in a bed with no supervision. My only colleague was a Frenchman, Raut, of whom I heard years afterwards, because he claimed to have possessed himself of the manuscript of a story by me which he was offering for sale. (I found myself unable to authenticate that manuscript.) Meals were served in a room upon a long table covered with American cloth and the food was poor and the cooking bad. There was neither time-table nor scheme of work. We started lessons just anyhow. Spasmodic unexpected half-holidays alternated with storms of educational energy, when we worked far into the evening. Jones had a certain gift for eloquence which vented itself in long prayers and exhortations at meals or on any odd occasion. He would open school with prayer. On occasions of crisis he would pray. His confidence in God was remarkable. He never hesitated to bring himself and us to the attention of an Avenging Providence. He did little teaching himself, but hovered about and interfered. At times, the tedium of life became too much for him and his wife. He would appear unexpectedly in the schoolroom, flushed and staggering, to make a long wandering discourse about nothing in particular or to assail some casual victim with vague disconcerting reproaches.

from *Experimenting in Autobiography* (1934)

Drowning in Wales
Philip Rock

Fenton sat in brooding silence during the ride to the railway station at Llangollen. It had started raining again and the dark hills and crags of North Wales looked sinister in the gloom. They barely caught the London-bound train as it stopped briefly on its run from Holyhead. The carriages were filled with Irish troops from County Down and Antrim, most of them sporting bits of orange cloth in their hatbands to show their contempt for the 'wearin' o' the green'. They were all in boisterous spirits. Out of training camp at last, heading for the war, 'Look out Kay-zer Bill!'

'Bloody idiots,' Fenton muttered as he slumped into a seat in a virtually empty first-class compartment. An Irish colonel and his adjutant were the only other occupants and the colonel glanced up curiously from a newspaper.

'Did you address me, sir?'

'No, sir, I did not. I was discussing the weather with my friend.'

'Yes. A man can drown in Wales when it rains. And the Taffies have the gall to say Belfast is wet!'

from *The Passing Bells* (1979)

County School Pride
Emyr Humphreys

The walls of Llanrhos County School, said Michael, are eloquent with its short history. This is Mr. Longwind James, first Chairman of the Governors, senior deacon at Moriah, a prominent tradesman, chairman of the Chamber of Commerce, town and county councillor, died 1917 (in bed). May the dust on the picture frame rest in peace. This still and silent group still displays the original pupils of the school, solemn unsmiling boys and girls of another century, in old clothes with young faces. The first headmaster sits in the middle, wearing a mortar-board and gown, a high, stiff collar and a drooping black moustache. This is a photograph taken at the opening ceremony; Lady M — key in hand, half turns to face the cameras, her smile lost in the shade of her immense wide hat. Her skirt brushes the steps leading to the front door. Aldermen, clergymen, unknown officials and their wives are also captured in the same frame. And here in faded sepia are the pupils of the school who were killed during the war of 1914-18, boys in uniform, with sad surprised faces.

In the Assembly Hall there is a Roll of Honour, said Albie, a black wooden image, stretching like a totem pole from the ceiling to the floor. Upon it there are names inscribed in gilt lettering, thus — John Ed. Jones, Burton School, U.C.N.W., 1899. This is the first name, at the top of the list; the last, almost on the floor, is Florence Hayes, Cohen Exhibition, Liver. University, 1907; and after her honourable pupils such as myself must pass without mention.

On either side of the dais at the end of the Assembly Hall are two large portraits; on the left, O. M. Edwards; on the right, Sir Herbert Lewis. The ruling headmaster stands between them, still liable to the law of change. We grow under his feet.

from *A Toy Epic* (1958)

Fishing on the Clwyd
George Melly

In 1935, for the first time Tom and Gampa took me fishing, something I'd begged them to do every year. We drove down a little lane one fine afternoon and Kane had to stop the car when a mother duck and about six babies in her wake emerged from the grass and waddled processionally across. We got to the fishing hut by the River Clwyd and Tom and Gampa put up three rods. They tied on flies for themselves and a big worm for me. I sat on the bank watching my float and listening to them bickering as they fished. Tom was the more impatient. He cast all the time. Gampa reproached him. 'What's the point of flogging the water, Tom? Wait for a rise.' I found it quite funny but a bit disorientating to hear my father told off like a small boy. Then my float bobbed. I did nothing. I knew from catching perch at Coniston that you didn't strike until it went under. It was most likely to be an eel. Gampa said I'd probably only catch eels. The float bobbed again a few times and then moved steadily down towards the bottom. I struck and gave an excited yelp as the rod bent double and the line came screaming off the reel. Tom and Gampa, shouting advice, ran towards me along the bank.

Twenty minutes later my first trout, three pounds in weight, lay on the grass in all its speckled glory. How responsible was I for landing it? Very little I should think, but they never took the rod off me. I believe my father stood behind me, his hands over mine, guiding them as to when to reel in, when to hold, when to let the fish run. Gampa netted it. When we got back to Hafod, Gampa wrote down in his fishing book:

DATE	RIVER	FISH	FLY	WEIGHT	REMARKS
Aug. 15 1935	Clwyd	Brown trout	worm	3lb.	G.M.'s first trout

from *Scouse Mouse* (1984)

Inside Denbigh Asylum
Caradog Pritchard

At last we came to a big gate at the side of the road and the motor car turned in through the gate and went along a wide gravelled path to the door of a great big place, four times the size of Salem chapel. There were stone steps on each side, leading up to the door.

'Sylum, I said to myself.

Dewi the Corner Shop's father came round to open the door for us, but Little Will Policeman's father stayed where he was, without moving. Mam was trembling like a leaf when she came out of the motor, but she didn't say anything, and the strange woman was gentle with her.

'You come with us now,' she said, and took my mother's arm. 'We'll just go and see the doctor and then everything will be all right.'

I followed after them, like a pet lamb.

A man in a white coat met us at the door after we'd climbed the stone steps, and he smiled as he welcomed us.

'Come through here to sit down while I go to fetch the nurse,' he told us and he took the strange woman and Mam and me into a sort of parlour, with a row of chairs along the wall and a table in the middle with a flower-pot on it full of flowers; there was a big window that you couldn't see through on the left side and on the right hand side there was a large cupboard with two doors to it. The three of us sat down on the chairs to wait.

We sat there for ages and the only thing that happened was Mam telling the strange woman that she wanted to go to the ladics' place. 'You come along with mc and I'll show you where it is,' the strange woman said kindly and they went out together, leaving me to sit on my own.

When they were away, a fat little man came in and, without taking any notice of me, he went up to the cupboard. After trying the door and finding it locked, he began to search his pockets for the key. First he went to his trouser pockets, but the key wasn't there, then he tried his waistcoat, then his jacket and then his breast pocket. But he didn't seem to have the key and in thc end he gave up and went out without opening the cupboard.

I thought he looked very much like my Uncle Will, but I was only imagining things, of course. After Mam and the strange woman came back, a pretty little girl in nurse's uniform came in, but she couldn't have been much older than me and she was smiling all over her face. Duw she was a pretty little piece, too, with her yellow hair and blue eyes and rosy cheeks. Her teeth shone white when she smiled at us. She had a big bunch of keys dangling from a piece of string in her hand. She looked just like little Jenny Pen Cae.

'Will you come with me, please' she asked Mam and the strange woman, but she took no notice of me. They both went with her and I stayed where I was.

I was feeling much more cheerful by then. I never thought the 'Sylum was a place like this, I said to myself. I expected to see a lot of lunatics. But suddenly I heard a horrible screech coming from the other side of that blind window and then a laugh rang out all over the place; I got up and went to the window, thinking about poor old Em. But I couldn't see through the window. Oh, it's only somebody playing a joke, I said to myself, and I went back to my chair.

In a while who should come in again but the same little fat man and he went straight to the cupboard, just like the first time, without taking a bit of notice of me. He started to go through his pockets to look for the key again and this time he found it in his waistcoat pocket. Once he had the cupboard door open, he took all sorts of rubbish out of it and piled everything into a heap on the floor. He seemed to be looking for something and failing to find it. After he'd emptied the cupboard, he put all the rubbish neatly back in again and turned the key in the lock. Then he put the key back into his pocket and went towards the door. But before he went out he stopped and turned to look at me. Then, very slowly, he walked back to me and stared at me in a very queer way.

'D'you know who I am?' he said.

No, I don't, I answered.

'I am the brother-in-law of Jesus Christ,' he told me.

Lord, I was scared. I didn't know whether to run for the door or laugh in his face.

Oh, indeed? I said in the end.

But he didn't say anything else; he turned on his heel and made to go out again. When he got to the door, he turned and said, without a smile on his face, 'In my Father's house there are many mansions'.

And out he went.

I killed myself laughing.

But I shut my mouth like a rat-trap when I saw a second man coming in and going to the cupboard. This one was a long thin man and his eyes seemed to have been sunk deep into his head. He only glanced at the cupboard and then he turned and came towards me.

'Did you see that man who came in just now?'

Yes, I said.

'He isn't all there, you know.'

Isn't he?

'Oh no, he's not sixteen ounces in the pound.' And out that one went as well. I got up and went to the window hoping to find a peep-hole in the white paint that covered it. But there wasn't one and I couldn't see anything. So I just sat again and waited. I was still having a quiet laugh about the two funny men, one so short and fat, and the other so long and thin.

In the end, the strange woman came back to the room, without my mother and carrying something in her hand.

'Here you are,' she said, 'you'll have to take these home with you.'

She put a small brown paper parcel tied with string into my hand.

What is it, then? I asked her.

'Your mother's clothes. And there are these, too. You'll have to take these as well.'

And she put the two rings in my other hand. One was Mam's wedding ring, worn thin, and the other one was the ring that had always been on my mother's finger.

I couldn't speak. I could only stare at the little parcel in my right hand and at the rings in my left. I kept trying to think how they could have got all Mam's clothes into such a small parcel.

It was then that I started to cry. But I didn't cry like I used to when I'd fallen and hurt myself long ago, and I didn't cry like I did at some funeral, nor the way I cried that time in Griff's bed when Mam went home and left me in Bwlch Farm years ago.

No, I was crying like throwing up.

Crying and not caring a damn who could see me.

Crying as if it were the end of the world.

Crying, howling, without a thought about who could hear me.

I enjoyed crying, like some people enjoy singing and others enjoy laughing.

Duw! I never cried like that before and I never have since, either. But I'd like to be able to cry like that just one more time.

I was still screaming crying as I went out through the door and down the stone steps and along the gravel path and through the gate to the road, till I sat down by the bank nor far from the gates. I stopped crying after a while and began to groan like a cow in calf. Then to howl crying, again.

from *Full Moon* (1961) trans. Menna Gallie

Mrs. Darby
Dewi Roberts

The mad woman came every Wednesday afternoon. Her name was Mrs. Darby and she was a patient at the local mental hospital.

Mrs. Darby looked mad, with her wild eyes and dishevelled black hair. A very grubby dress which looked as though it had been obtained at thirdhand from a charity, completed her unruly appearance. She was allowed the freedom to walk in the local countryside and to visit the nearest town. On one of her rural rambles she met my parents and during the course of a conversation revealed a passion for popular music.

'I wish I 'ad a piano to practise on,' she said plaintively. 'It 'ud be a Godsend to me would a piano. I can't play no piano, stuck in the "big 'ouse" up there,' and she gestured in the general direction of the hospital. The 'big 'ouse' was a term frequently used by patients and local people in referring to the hospital.

My ever-hospitable parents quickly agreed that Mrs. Darby should be allowed to practise on the piano in the kitchen of our small cottage. She proved to be a manic pianist, the same item being hammered out time and time again: 'It's a Grand Night for Singing,' still thunders through my head. She hit an incredible number of wrong notes and the resulting cacophony was deafening. Mother would stand in the kitchen doorway with a bemused expression on her face. Perhaps she saw Mrs. Darby as the catalyst in a conspiracy to make *her* mad too.

On one of her visits Mrs. Darby seemed more volatile than usual and Mother soon learned the reason for this. Over a cup of tea, Mrs. Darby said that she had started courting Jack Evans, a labourer on a large farm in the area. Jack was a simple minded, inoffensive man.

'My Jack's a wonderful fella,' she enthused. 'All these wasted years rotting in the "big 'ouse" and I should have been with Jack, but now he'll give me everything I've ever wanted when we get married.'

Mrs. Darby and Jack would be seen walking on leafy lanes on summer evenings, or standing on the river bank staring into the reflective stillness of the water. Inevitably this led to gossip.

'I seen Jack an' that mental patient up at the Graig today.'

'What were they doing?'

'Holdin' hands.'

'Well I don't suppose it stopped at holding hands.'

The general conclusion of such gossip was that no possible good could emerge from their relationship. As it happened, it was justified. For a period of weeks Mrs. Darby was no longer seen in the area and my parents could not understand why her visits had so suddenly come to an end. Eventually rumours were related to them, and they were deeply shocked. It seemed that an abortion on Mrs. Darby had been carried out in the hospital.

The immense trauma of this experience on a woman who was already sick resulted in her becoming wild to the point of violence. She was said to have punched and bitten some of the staff, and attempted to take her own life in one of the toilets. It came as no surprise to discover that she had been transferred from an unlocked ward to one were security was rigorous.

'That poor sick woman,' my mother said, feelingly, 'just think what she's gone through . . . my heart goes out to her.'

'The Lord will find a purpose behind it,' responded Father with a Victorian sense of detachment.

'Memories' from *Reminiscences of Clwyd*, (ed Joan Owusu 1993)

Twenty-four Pairs of Socks
Emyr Humphreys

In the chest of drawers there are two dozen pairs of warm socks.
The man who wore them had the secret of living.
He was prepared at any time to say what it was
so that as far as he was concerned
it was no secret.

When he lived I could not think
that what he believed brought him peace and happiness,
was the true source of content.
If he said FAITH I remembered his ulcer.
Whether installed by heredity or induced by anxiety
an ulcer is surely something that nags,
coaxed to grow in a greenhouse of despair.

If he modestly implied GOOD WORKS by his concern for others
and his unswerving devotion to political idealism of the most naive
kind
I would like to point out that he never cleaned his own boots until
his wife died
and as far as I know
no party he voted for or supported ever stood in danger
of being obliged to exercise power.

Sometimes his calm was unnerving.
At others, one sock of a pair missing, or some such trifle
he would tremble and then erupt, —
the burst of red-faced fury
of an angry peasant cheated at a fair.

But mostly he was calm. Nearly always.

(Not counting a certain tremolo when he was swept with righteous
indignation.)

It was generally accepted that he was a good man,
and it pleased him deeply to know that his visits were welcomed.
In the wards his presence, his nod and bow especially,
did everyone a lot of good.

Everything about him suggested that the secret was not his own
but something given, something to share that came from a source
outside —
available to all like the warmth of the sun and words.

He was a preacher of course.
The drawers of his desk are packed so tight with sermons
they refuse to open.
His three suits or clerical grey hang in the little wardrobe.
In the chest of drawers there are twenty-four pairs of warm socks.

Ancestor Worship (1970)

Saliwt (Salute)
Euros Bowen

(In memory of William Alwyn Jones and George Taylor, Abergele.)

Bedeck both coffins
red, green, and white,
with the colours of our country's honour.

Bear the silence of their flesh
between the pacing of respect before them
and the pride that strides behind,
and at the roadside,
shoulder to shoulder,
let the leaves
of sycamore and ash and oak bow,
for
our age never sensed

the scent of blood so strange
as the aura of these remains.

Beat upon the dullness of the drums
the dirge of marching
to the tombs' domain
in the holy freedom of the land.

trans. Frank Olding

[William Alwyn Jones and George Taylor were killed in an abortive attempt to assassinate Prince Charles shortly before the Investiture in 1969]

History

Pontnewydd Cave, Valley of the Elwy
Gladys Mary Coles

These trowels unlock the earth
deftly lift wedges like chocolate gateau
chink on clinker, cola cans
the flat tongues of flint.

Within the cave's cool dark, again
men and women cluster, crouch
over prehistoric fires, forage
for likely bones, appropriate stones.

Excited by a possibility, they chunter
sifting the soil tenderly, harvesting
fragments of something, someone —
the worn milk tooth of a child, born
a quarter of a million years before the Nazarene,
an adult's ground-down molar
bones of a bear's forearm
the flakes of tools, leaf-shaped spearheads.

Satisfied, they seal the sepulchre,
depart with their hunting equipment:
silence reclaims the hillside
where, high above the wooded valley,
limestone reflects sunlight, signals
to the tawny Elwy as it slides
seeking the once-carboniferous sea.

from *The Glass Island* (1992)

The Bronze Age in Denbighshire
Dr. Frances Lynch

The history of man as a hunter in Denbighshire is well recorded, both before and after the last Ice Age, but our knowledge of the first farmers in the area is rather more uncertain because the tradition of building large stone tombs was not as well-established here as it was in the west. But towards the end of the Neolithic, about 2500 BC, evidence of human settlement in north east Wales becomes clearer, for man begins to occupy new territory — to farm the higher ground. This may have been because the old lands were exhausted or because of more complex social changes. The introduction of new metal technology and a more individualistic attitude in society used to be attributed to invaders from the Continent [Beaker Folk] but the transformation of native society is now seen as more complex and more akin to the changes wrought in sixteenth century Britain than to the Norman conquest. These changes are most clearly seen in graves. Several of the new single graves are known from the county, people buried with a characteristic Beaker pot. Later generations are often buried in the same mound, as at Plas Heaton, Henllan, or cemeteries such as that at Brenig may be constructed.

The Brenig cemetery contained not only burial monuments but also a ceremonial site, the Ring Cairn, which was used for up to five hundred years for ceremonies which, though probably connected with funerals, involved the burial of charcoal, not human bone. The community in the Brenig valley was not rich, but they traded with people in Yorkshire who shared many of their religious and social ideas. In the north people were not buried with weapons in the way that they were in the south and, even when they were rich, like the man who wore the Mold Cape, their regalia was not a military one.

Some people in North Wales may have become very rich through their manufacture of bronze tools. The region has natural resources such as copper and lead (but not tin) and recent work has shown that the mines on the Great Orme date back to this period. The bronzesmiths of Denbighshire were also in the forefront of experimentation, designing a more effective axehead and using an unusual, but very tough metal mix which added a little lead to the more normal tin and copper. A group of tools from Moelfre Uchaf, Betws-yn-Rhos, shows the experimental stage of this industry and another find from Acton Park, Wrexham, contains the fully developed style of North Welsh Palstave. These tools have been found exported to north Germany, Holland and Brittany.

But though we can say a lot about the metal industry and traditions of burial, it is still difficult to point to living sites, to the farms which supported this society. At Brenig, analysis of the vegetation from the old ground surface and from the mounds showed that arable fields existed nearby, but the excavation did not find them. These upland farms may have been ruined by the worsening of the climate at about 1100 BC. All over Britain there is evidence for the abandonment of fields and farms on the moors at this time and it is likely that famine and disease stalked the land.

However, the one group of Bronze Age farms (perhaps only hafodau) found on Hiraethog, those at Bryn Helen, near Pentre Llyn Cymer, show that the population recovered quite quickly, for they date from about 1000 BC. Certainly, by the Early Iron Age, someone near Cerrig-y-Drudion was wealthy enough to import a fine bronze bowl from the Continent — but that is another story.

Denbigh History Society (1993)

The Ordouices
John Speede

The ancient inhabitants of this County were the Ordouices, who are also named Ordeuices, or Ordouice: a courteous and courageous people by reason of they kept wholly in a mountain place and took heart even of the soil itself: for they continued longest free from the yoke both of Roman and also of English dominion.They were not subdued by the Romans before the days of the Emperor Domitian (for then Julius Agricola conquered the whole Nation) nor brought under the command of the English before the reign of King Edward the First; but lived a long time in a lawless kind of liberty as bearing themselves bold upon their own magnaminity and the strength of the County.

from *Theatre of the Empire of Great Britain* (1610)

Bangor Iscoed
W. Watkin Davies

From Wrexham we may also pay a visit to Bangor Iscoed, a place not to be confused with the better known Bangor on the shores of the Menai Straits. In olden days 'Bangor' meant Bangor Iscoed. The little village of Bangor-on-Dee stands, as its name implies, on the bank of the Dee, and a picturesque bridge there spans the river. It is said that the Roman town of Bovium once stood there. At all events there was established one of the first monasteries in Britain. Bangor Iscoed was celebrated throughout the whole Christian world. There Pelagius, the famous heretic and bitter opponent of St. Augustine, lived in the fourth century, though he was not a monk. Tragedy overtook the monastery in the year 607. The Britons of Wales just then were contesting every inch of ground against the invading English. One of those heathen English, King Ethelfrith of Northumbria, advanced against Bangor, and there fought a great battle. While the battle was in progress, the monks of the neighbouring monastery, numbering more than twelve hundred, stood by praying for the success of the Christian army and for the defeat of the pagans. Ethelfrith must have been a clear-headed fellow, for he saw at once that this sort of prayer must be considered contraband of war, a sort of conduct that *ipso facto* ranged the monks with combatants. 'Those who pray against me fight against me', he shouted; and thereupon gave orders for the whole twelve hundred monks to be slain, and the monastery razed to the ground. Only a few of them escaped the massacre: and they betook themselves, together with their piety and their culture, to the remote island of Bardsey, where they would be perfectly safe from all possibility of English persecution.

from *A Wayfarer in Wales* (1930)

Owain Glyndwr at Sycharth
Thomas Pennant

Writers vary in the account of the day of the birth of *Glyndwr*. One manuscript fixes it on the 28th of *May* 1354: that preserved by *Lewis Owen* places the event five years earlier; for the year 1349, says he, was distinguished by the first appearance of the pestilence in *Wales*, and by the birth of *Owen Glyndwr*.

Heroes are often introduced into the world by some strange phenomenon, that presages their future celebrity, or the happiness or misery they were to bring upon their country; but it is probable that their course is finished, before superstition invents the tale, and adapts it to their actions. *Holinshed* relates one on this occasion, correspondent to a blemish from which we could wish to clear the character of our countryman. His cruelty was foretold at his nativity, by the marvellous accident of his father's horses being found standing that night in the stables up to their bellies in blood. *Shakespear* omits this circumstance; but, in his spirited character of Owen, puts these beautiful lines into his mouth, finely descriptive of the vain-glory and superstition of the old *British* chieftain.

At *my* birth
The front of heav'n was full of fiery shapes;
The goats ran from the mountains, and the herds
Were strangely clamorous in the frighted fields:
These signs have mark'd me extraordinary,
And all the courses of my life do shew,
I am not in the roll of the common men.

His bard, *Jolo Goch*, gives him incense of a far superior kind; and I fear the poet's ardor to celebrate his patron, carried him to the borders of blasphemy; for, in his *Cowydd y Seren*, or *Poem of the star*, he describes three that appeared to mark three great events; for, to the star which foretold the birth of our SAVIOUR, he adds another which presaged that of *Arthur*; and a third which marked the great deeds of *Glyndwr*, in 1402, the meridian of his glory.

He appears to have had a liberal education. His ambition overcame the prejudices of his country against the *English*; and determined him to seek preferment among them. He entered himself in the inns of court, and studied there, till he became a barrister. It is probable that he quitted his profession; for we find, that he was appointed *scutiger*, or squire of the body, to *Richard* II whose fortunes he followed to the last; was taken with him in *Flint* castle; and, when the king's household was dissolved, retired, with full resentment of his sovereign's wrongs, to his patrimony in *Wales*. I judge that he was knighted before the deposition of his master; for I find him among the witnesses in the celebrated cause between Sir *Richard le Scrope* and Sir *Robert le Grosvenour*, about a coat of arms, under the title of Sir *Owen de Glendore*. His brother also appears there by the name of *Tudor de Glendore*. This cause lasted three years, and ended in 1389.

Jolo Goch, the celebrated poet of this period, resided here for some time. He came on a pressing invitation from *Owen*; who, knowing the mighty influence of this order of men over the antient *Britons*, made his house, as *Jolo* says a sanctuary for bards. He made them the instruments of his future operations, and to prepare the minds of the people against the time of his intended insurrection. From *Jolo* I borrow the description of the seat of the chieftain, when it was in full splendor. He compares it, in point of magnificence, to *Westminster* abbey; and informs us, that it had a gatehouse, and was surrounded with a moat.

That within were nine halls, each furnished with a wardrobe; I imagine, filled with the cloaths of his retainers, according to the custom of those days.

Near the house, on a verdant bank, was a wooden house, supported on posts, and covered with tiles. It contained four apartments, each subdivided into two, designed to lodge the guests.

Here was a church, in form of a cross, with several chapels.

The seat was surrounded with every conveniency for good living; and every support to hospitality: a park, warren, and pigeon-house; a mill, orchard, and vine-yard; and fish-pond, filled with pike and gwyniads. The last introduced from the lake at *Bala*.

A heronry, which was a concomitant to the seat of every great man, supplied him and his guests with game for the sport of falconry.

A place still remains, that retains the name of his park. It extends about a mile or two beyond the site of his house, on the left hand of the valley.

The vestiges of the house are small. The moat is very apparent: the measurement of the area it inclosed, is forty-six paces by twenty-six. There is the appearance of a wall on the outside, which was continued to the top of a great mount, on which stood the wooden house. On the other side, but at a greater distance, I had passed by another mount of the same kind, called *Hendom*; which probably might have had formerly a building similar to that described by the bard. This, perhaps, was the station of a guard, to prevent surprize or insult from the *English* side. He had much to apprehend from the neighboring fortress of *Dinas Brân*, and its appendages, possessed by the earl of *Arundel*, a strenuous supporter of the house of *Lancaster*.

The bard speaks feelingly of the wine, the ale, the braget, and the white bread; nor does he forget the kitchen, nor the important officer the cook; whose life (when in the royal service) was estimated by our laws at a hundred and twenty-six cows.

Such was the hospitality of this house, that the place of porter was useless; nor were locks or bolts known. To sum up all, no one could be hungry or dry in *Sycharth*, the name of the place.

from *Tours in Wales* (1778-1781)

Glyndwr's Home
Iolo Goch

'Tis water girdled wide about
It shows a wide and stately door
Reached by a bridge the water o'er
'Tis formed of buildings coupled fair,
Coupled is every couple there;
Within a quadrate structure tall,
Master the merry pleasures all.
Co-jointly are the angles bound —
No flaw in all the place is found.
Structures in contact meet the eye
Upon the hillocks top on high;
Into each other fastened they
The form of a hard knot display.
There dwells the chief we all extoll
In timber house on lightsome knoll
Upon four wooden columns proud
Each column thick and firmly bas'd
And upon each a loft is placed;
In these four lofts which coupled stand
Repose at night the minstrel band;
Four lofts they were in pristine state
But now, partitioned, form they eight.
Tiled is the roof, on each house top
Rise smoke-ejecting chimneys up
All of one form there are nine halls
Each with nine wardrobes within its walls
With linen white as well supplied
As fairest shops in famed Cheapside
Behold that church with cross upraised
And with its windows neatly glazed.
All houses are in this comprest —
An orchard's near it of the best.
Also a park where void of fear
Feed antlered herds of fallow deer.
A warren wide my chief can boast.
Of goodly steeds a countless host.
Meads where for hay the clover grows,

Cornfields which hedges trim enclose
A mill a rushing brook upon,
And pigeon tower fram'd of stone.
A fishpond deep and dark to see
To cast nets in when need there be
Which never yet was known to lack
A plenteous store of perch and jack
Of various plumage birds abound
Herons and peacocks haunt around
What luxury doth his hall adorn
Showing of cost a sovereign scorn
His ale from Shrewsbury town he brings.
His usquebagh is drink for kings;
Bragget he keeps, bread white of look
And, bless the mark, a bustling cook
His mansion is the minstrel's home
You'll find them there whene'er you come
Of all her sex his wife's the best;
The household through her care is blest;
She's scion of a knightly tree,
She's dignified, she's kind and free
His bairns approach me, pair by pair,
Oh what a nestful of chieftains there
Here difficult it is to catch
A sight of either bolt or latch
The porters place here none will fill;
Here largesse shall be lavished still
And ne'er shall thirst or hunger rude
In Sycharth venture to intrude.
A noble leader, Cambria's knight,
The lake possesses, his by right
And in that azure water placed
The castle by each pleasure grac'd.

trans. George Borrow

An Enduring Heritage
T.E. Ellis

It was not from a borough or a garrison town but from one of the glens of the Dee that Owen Glyndwr rose to wage his fifteen years' memorable struggle for Wales. Huw Morris, Pont y Meibion, and Morgan Llwyd o Wynedd, the two Welsh voices of the seventeenth century, were country folk. So were all the leaders of the religious revival. Thomas Charles and Lewis Edwards came from peasant hearths. Diosg Farm sheltered the three famous brothers of Llanbrynmair, pioneers of Welsh reform. William Rees and Henry Rees, who from this city wielded so strong and noble an influence over their countrymen, were nurtured at Chwibren Issa, in the free bracing air of the Hiraethog hills. From cottages nestling under the Berwyns have sprung typical men like Ceiriog, Ieuan Gwynedd, and Owen Edwards. And there is no reason to suppose that the country districts will cease to form the nursery ground of men of thought, initiative, and influence.

from *Speeches and Addresses* (1912)

The Saxons of Flint
Lewis Glyn Cothi

A man, like others, formed by God,
On Sunday morning last I trod
The street of Flint, an ill-built maze,
I wish the whole were in a blaze.
An English marriage feast was there
Which, like all English feasts, was spare.
Naught there revealed our mountain land,
The generous heart, the liberal hand.
No tankard there was passed around
With richly-foaming mead high-crowned.
The reason why I thither came,
Was something for my art to claim.
An art that oft from prince and lord
Has won its just, it's due reward.

With lips inspired I then began,
To sing an ode to this mean clan.
Rudely they mocked my song and me,
And loathed my oft-praised minstrelsy.
Alas, that through my cherished art
Boors should distress and wound my heart.

Fool that I was to think the muse
Could charm corn-dealers — knavish Jews.
My polished ode forsooth they hissed
And I midst laughter was dismissed.
For William Beiser's bag they bawl.
'Largess for him!' they loudly call.
Each roared with throat at widest stretch
For Will the Piper — low born wretch.
Will forward steps — as best he can,
Unlike a free, enobled man.
A pliant bag 'tween arm and chest,
While limping on, he tightly prest.
He stares — he strives — the bag to sound,
He swells his maw — and ogles round.
He twists and turns himself about.
With fetid breath his cheeks swell out.
What savage boors! His hideous claws
And glutton's skin win their applause.
With shuffling hand and hideous mien
To doff his coat he next is seen.
He snorted, bridled in his face
And bent it down with much grimace.
Like to a kite he seemed that day.
The churl did blow a grating shriek.
The bag did swell and harshly squeak.
As does a goose from a nightmare crying
Or dog, crushed by a chest, when dying.
the whistling box's changeless note
Is forced from turgid vein and throat.
The sound is like the crane's harsh moan
Or like a gosling's latest groan.
Just such a noise a wounded goat
Sends from hoarse and gurgling throat.
His unattractive, screeching lay

Being ended, William sought for pay.
Some fees he had from this mean band,
But largess from no generous hand.
Some pence were offered by a few.
Others gave little halfpence too.
Unheeded by this shabby band,
I left the feast with empty hand.
A dire mischance I wish indeed,
On slavish Flint and its mean breed.
Oh, may its furnace be the place
Which they and their piper Will may grace.
For their ill-luck my prayer be told,
My curses on them, young and old!
If once again I venture there.
May death a second visit spare.

trans. M.C. Llewelyn

Lewis Glyn Cothi (c. 1420-89), acknowledged as one of the major fifteenth century poets, once attended a wedding reception in Flint. he assumed that the guests would be captivated by his ballad singing. But unfortunately those present were English and they dismissed Cothi, calling instead for another man to entertain them on the bagpipes. This ballad reflects the deep antipathy between Wales and England during the early period of the Tudor dynasty.

The Elwy Valley
S. Baring Gould

The Cefn caves are in an escarpment of mountain limestone high above the river, and have been carefully explored. They yielded bones of extinct animals — the cave bear, wolf, *elephas antiqitus*, *bos longifrons*, reindeer, the hyaena, and the rhinoceros — but very scanty traces of man. The bones are preserved at Plas-yn-Cefn, the residence of Mrs. Williams-Wynn, on whose property the caves are. The caves are worth visiting more for the view from the rocks than for any intrinsic interest in themselves.

A quaint Elizabethan mansion, Plas Newydd, has in its wainscoted hall an inscription to show that it was built by one Foulk ab Robert in 1583 when he was aged forty-three. It is said to have been the first house in the neighbourhood covered with slates. A giant, Cawr Rhufoniog, used to visit there, and a crook is shown high up near the cornice, on which he was wont to suspend his hat. Giants, it would appear, were in days of yore pretty plentiful in this neighbourhood. The grave of one is pointed out close by, and another, Edward Shon Dafydd, otherwise called Cawr y Ddôl, lived at an adjoining farm. His walking-stick was the axle-tree of a cart, with a huge crowbar driven into one end and bent for a handle. He and Sir John Salusbury (of the double thumbs) once fell to testing their strength by uprooting forest trees.

Between Plas Newydd and Plas-yn-Cefn, in a field, is a 'covered avenue,' only it has lost all its coverers. It was in a mound called Carnedd Tyddyn Bleiddyn, with some trees on the top. When these were blown down in a storm, a little over thirty years ago, the cromlech within was exposed. It was found to contain several skeletons, in a crouching position, of what have been called the Platycnemic Men of Denbighshire

from *A Book of North Wales* (1903)

A Plea to Sir Bribem

Gwyn Williams

The Elizabethan ironworks should not be thought of as something localised . . . .

They were small and there were two hundred of them in Wales in 1613. And they moved about. When all the woods in the district had been cut down and burnt the furnace was picked up and rebuilt in a new, unspoiled area. The popular poets expressed what the Welsh people thought of this stripping of their woodlands, and the extent of the deprivation which resulted from this destruction of an environment is amusingly detailed by a wandering poet of the lower order, a *clerwr* called Robin Clidro, in a 'poem on behalf of the squirrels who went to London to file and make an affidavit on the bill for the cutting down of Marchan Wood, near Rhuthun'. I translate part of what their leader, a matronly red squirrel, says on oath to the Bailiff, whom she refers to as Sir Bribem:

All Rhuthun's woods are ravaged;
my house and barn were taken
one dark night, and all my nuts.
The squirrels are all calling
for the trees; they fear the dog.
Up there remains of the hill wood
only grey ash of oak-trees;
there's not a stump unstolen
nor a crow's nest left in our land.
The owls are all the time hooting
for trees, they send the children mad.
The poor owl catches cold,
left cold without her hollow trunk.

from *A Land Remembers* (1977)

The Perils of Mining
Richard Warner

Perilous as the business of mining appears to be, one naturally expects to hear of frequent accidents among the workmen. Habit, however, renders them so expert, that *serious* casualties seldom occur. Some 'hair-breadth-escapes', indeed, are on record, which, had they not been told us by those whose veracity is unquestionable, we should not have very hastily given credit to. Of these the following are most remarkable:

A few years since a workman fell down the shafts of a mine in the neighbourhood of Holywell, nearly one hundred and twenty feet deep, and was so little incommoded by the sudden descent as to exclaim to his companions above, who were anticipating his immediate death, 'Ecod, I've broke my *clogs*'.

A coachman of Mr. Pennant, also, fell down a coal-pit, with similar good fortune.

These, however, were nothing, when compared to the adventure of a man now living at Whiteford, near Holywell, who, when a lad tumbled into one of these mines, of *three hundred feet*, and escaped alive.

Not more than two or three years since, the roof of a neighbouring mine gave way so suddenly, that a poor workman, not having time to escape, was instantly overwhelmed with the foundering earth. Standing fortunately at this time under a mass of rock, he escaped being immediately crushed to death; but as there were many thousand tons of earth above him, the melancholy prospect of certain destruction, by means the most lingering and terrible, still presented itself to him. When the accident happened, he had half a pound of candles in his hand, and upon this, and the trickling water that distilled through the cracks of the rock, he subsisted nine days, until his faithful companions, who, with an anxious solicitude that does honour to humanity, worked incessantly (spell and spell) for nine days and as many nights, at length reached, and liberated him from the horrible prison in which he was immured.

A singular instance of providential preservation occurred yesterday, also, in a coal-mine at Mostyn park, a few miles from the scene of the last wonder. As *twelve* men were following their employment in the dark recesses of the mountain, the water suddenly burst and in a few minutes must have overwhelmed them all. The rope, however, by which the bucket is drawn up, happened to be hanging down at this critical moment, and the whole party clinging to it, hallooed lustily to their companions above to pull them up. Their cries were heard, and the people immediately wound up the rope, which brought them safely to the top, though it had that very day been deemed as too old and unsafe to be longer used.

from *A Second Walk Through Wales*, (1798)

The High Price of Corn
David Jones

Large mobs frequently assembled early in 1795 because of the high price of corn. The magistrates found it more and more difficult to restrain them until, at Mold, a mob broke open the warehouse of a dealer who exported corn to Cheshire and Lancashire, and forced him to sell it at something under the market price. It was found necessary to call for troops. 'At present', wrote one Flintshire magistrate to the Home Office, 'there are none in this Country or near it, and should the numerous body of Colliers and Miners again assemble, the property of the whole country might be laid waste and destroy'd before Assistance could be procured.'

On 1 April a spectacular disturbance caused dismay in the town of Denbigh. A mob of several hundreds rioted against new conscription demands and imprisoned three justices of the peace. Some of the rioters then marched north-west to Rhuddlan, where they intended to unload any corn ready loaded for export. On hearing the news of these disturbances, the Duke of York immediately ordered cavalry to Denbigh, but rioting still continued. On 10 April between three and four hundred people descended on the town of Abergele, armed with homemade weapons, and assaulted a man who had warned a group of workmen a month previously not to join a corn riot. Later in April it was feared that four thousand people might rise and march on Denbigh. The government was persuaded to keep the existing military force in the town, and also to send some troops to Ruthin. With the presence of the military, the peace of the area seems to have been restored.

from *Before Rebecca: Popular Protests in Wales* (1973)

Sister Rebecca
Harry Tobit Evans

On 20 November the Mardy Toll-Gate, within five miles of Corwen, on the Holyhead road, in the parish of Llangwm (Denbigh), and belonging to the Bala Trust, was entirely taken away. The posts were parted with a saw, and a note put under the door informing the toll-keeper that the breach was committed by Sister Rebecca, with a caution against placing another in that neighbourhood.

from *Rebecca and Her Daughters* (1910)

The Battle of Cinder Hill
George G. Lerry

The Ruabon Riots occurred in December 1830. The principal cause of the disturbances which took place was the Truck System under which miners and other workers had to take their wages in kind from the 'Truck' or 'Tommy' shops owned by the Colliery proprietors. The men were bound to take cheese, bacon, wheat, etc., from these shops and often had to sell the goods served out to them in lieu of wages, to other people in order to obtain the money they needed for other necessities of life. Protest meetings against the Truck System were held all over the district without effecting any change, and so the miners of Cefn, Acrefair, Rhos, Brymbo and other places went on strike. A large crowd of colliers and other workers from several districts met at Rhos and were said to be bent on destroying the Truck Shop attached to the Acrefair Ironworks. The Denbighshire Yeomanry were called out and assembled at Rhos. Sir Watkin Williams-Wynn, Major Edward Lloyd Lloyd, and the Vicar of Ruabon, Rev. Rawland Wingfield, spoke to the men and tried to persuade them to return home.

'Sir Watkin,' according to the Yeomanry records, 'promised to interview the masters and endeavour to do away with the objectionable 'truck' system if the rioters would disperse peaceably, and there is no doubt that this appeal might have been quite successful had it not been for the fact that the constables had received orders from the magistrates to arrest several of the ringleaders, and as the mob showed a disposition to resist them, the Yeomanry Cavalry had to patrol the streets of the place in order to 'terrify' the rioters. As soon as the mob, aided by the presence of the mounted force, had quietened down and showed no disposition for further violence, the Denbighshire Yeomanry started on their return journey from Rhos, passing through Gutter Hill.

By the side of the road at this place there was a large mound of cinders, the refuse of the neighbouring blast furnace. On this mound, which was above the level of the road, some thousands of persons were standing looking at the Yeomanry as they defiled past, on their way to the turnpike road at Ruabon. When the Cavalry were nearly past the cinder mound a youth threw a piece of cinder at the passing troops, and the missile striking one of the horses made it jump.

The owner of the horse and his comrade at once drew their pistols and fired at the persons on the mound.

Sir Watkin, who was riding at the head of the regiment, was very indignant, and severely reprimanded the two troopers for their silly and dangerous act.

Fortunately no one was hurt, though the balls, it was said, were heard by some people on the mound whizzing past their heads, and what was still more fortunate, Sir Watkin, by his prompt action in checking the men, saved a fierce conflict with the colliers, who were much enraged by this act.

The colliers now returned to their homes and the Denbighshire Yeomanry were dismissed from duty. This affair, which as time went on became much magnified was known locally as the 'Battle of Cinder Hill'.

from *The Collieries of Denbighshire* (1946)

The Coastal Line
Askew Roberts

When a railway between Chester and Holyhead was first projected, there were not wanting those who heartily condemned a line along the coast, arguing that Telford had shown the best route to Ireland. However, the coast line projectors won the day, and vigorously prosecuted their works, but before the winter of 1847 had passed the unopened railway and sea walls in some places were washed away. Then the objectors came again to the front, and we were solemnly warned by our watchful guardians, the newspapers, that frightful would be the slaughter on this hazardous undertaking. Nevertheless, so far as we know, there has never been an accident caused by slipping of the line into the sea, although there are times when 'The Wild Irishman' has to exercise extra caution. In 1872 this highly paced traveller was brought to a standstill by signal rockets between Mostyn and Prestatyn because the sea wall had given way; and at the beginning of 1877 a detour by way of St. Asaph was occasioned by the inroads of the sea.

from The Gossiping Guide to Wales (1881)

A Railway Catastrophe
Roderick O'Flanagan

We left Llandudno and its attractions, to seek others, on our way to London. Proceeding onward towards Abergele, we reached a small station — Llandulas — which has a melancholy interest for me — one of the most terrible in the ghastly record of railway catastrophes, and they are appalling enough.

On August 19, 1968, the Hon. Judge Berwick and his sister look places in the Irish limited mail, *en route* for Ireland. The Judge had been on the Continent for the benefit of his health, and as I was then one of the officials of the Court of Bankruptcy in Dublin, of which he was Judge, Mr. Connellan, my colleague, who for many years was the trusted and most intimate friend and agent for Judge Berwick, told me he received a letter from him, stating: 'If any one is expecting my place, he must wait for it, as my health is quite re-established, and I expect to be in Court on August 20'. In the carriage with Judge and Miss Berwick were Lord and Lady Farnham, Sir Broderick and Lady Chinnery, and a little girl, of whom Judge and Miss Berwick had taken charge for her friends in Dublin. The train had proceeded at its wonted speed till nearing Llandulas, where it was met by some trucks which unfortunately broke away from a goods train while being shunted to allow the mail train to pass. These trucks contained barrels of petroleum, and from the collision the petroleum ignited and set the nearest carriages in a blaze. A woman rushed to the carriage in which my friends sat, and called on them in excited tones 'to throw out the child, as the carriage was on fire'. The survivors say 'the shock was so slight that no one could realize the danger until it was too late,' for in almost a minute the flames caught the body of the carriage, and then all was over. Twenty-eight persons were burnt to death, among them all those I have mentioned . . . .

A monument in the churchyard of Abergele records this sad event.

from *Through North Wales With My Wife* (1884).

Troubled Times
A *Times* Correspondent

I entered Denbighshire in the fond hope of discovering that the chances of violence in the future were decreasing, and that the people were settling down into those orderly habits of life which are suited to their national character. But there is no ground for indulging in any such hope. Those who know the county and its inhabitants well are agreed that the danger of the situation cannot be easily exaggerated. They are convinced that men either will not or dare not pay their tithes, and that the agitation will soon extend, if it has not already extended, to the payment of rent also. They are certain that each new attempt to enforce the law will be met with increased violence and disorder. Into the actual condition of the questions affecting the tithe and the land, into the relations between Churchmen and Dissenters in Wales, into the state of agriculture, and so on, I must enter later, since there is first a great personage, those character and position Englishmen will not readily appreciate, to be dealt with at some length. In spite of an inveterate hatred for personalities, it is impossible to avoid the mention of the name of the man who is, as far as I have been able to ascertain, the responsible source and cause of the troubles which have agitated Wales during recent times, exerting over his fellow-countrymen an extraordinary influence. That man is Mr. Thomas Gee, of Denbigh. Into the details of his early life it is unnecessary to enter; it is enough to say that since 1857 he has been the proprietor, and it is believed the real editor, of far the most influential of Welsh papers, *Baner ac Amserau Cymru* (the Banner and Times of Wales). In that position he has shown consistency upon at least one point; he has never missed an opportunity of opposing the very existence of the Church of England in Wales, and he may safely be regarded as the originator of the anti-tithe movement. Upon this matter he expresses himself with some force. His son, acting as his mouthpiece, informed Mr. Commissioner Bridge that 'many tenants went to his father with tears in their eyes, and begged him to help them in their distress consequent upon the fall in agricultural prices and the heavy and unequal tithes they were called upon to pay'.

Mr. Gee also wrote to Mr. Bridge as follows:

> The agitation has arisen from a deep-rooted objection to the principle of an Establishment — a feeling which is greatly intensified by the fact that it is an alien Church, and includes but a small minority of the inhabitants. The payment of tithes to this Church is a badge of conquest which we are determined to shake off as soon as possible. The present state of agriculture is not the cause but the occasion of this agitation, the farmers having been obliged to look for reduction both in rent and tithe to save themselves from further ruin. They are fully justified in appealing to the clergy for reductions as well as to the landowners, not withstanding their contracts. The tithe is not a tax

upon the land, but upon its produce, and thereby upon the brains, the capital, and the industry of the tenant farmer . . . .

As the Ecclesiastical Commissioners have so grossly insulted and exasperated my fellow-countrymen by calling for the assistance of the military and police to protect them while securing the full payment of their tithes under the above conditions, their conduct can never be forgotten.

from *Letters from Wales* (1889)

Dispute and Conflict
Trevor Herbert

There was also a history of intermittent dispute and conflict, sometimes violent, in the other extractive industries of north Wales. The coal-mining industry of north-east Wales had a long association with trade *unionism*, and an experience of struggle most tragically displayed in the Mold 'riots' of 1869 which had claimed the lives of two colliers and two women shot by the military. But there had been clashes, too, of differing levels of seriousness between other workers and their employers: in Llanddulas itself Fusiliers from Chester had been brought into the village in 1829 to quell rebellious limestone quarrymen who were opposing the enclosure of common land. Strikes were also common in the lead and copper mines of north Wales, particularly in response to employers' attempts to lengthen the hours of work, and change the nature of the wages system: Halkyn miners rioted in 1822 and in 1850 miners armed with sticks won a reduction of hours in Holywell . . . .

The workers of the extractive industries of north Wales, therefore, were not unfamiliar with industrial struggle and the tactics of direct action, tactics which they employed in defence of their working conditions, their wages, or their hours of work.

from *People and Protest: Wales 1815-1880* (1988)

A Tithe Riot

A Reporter

On Thursday Stephens left Denbigh with eight bailiffs and thirty police officers. This imposing assembly was energetically hooted on their departure in their carriages. When they reached Llannefydd there was a crowd of about 1,000 waiting to welcome them with loud hoots, groans, and fearful screams. These were supplemented by blowing horns, beating pitchers, or any other instrument capable of making a noise.The crowd was determined to thwart the activities of Stephens and his men and efforts were made to separate them and trip them up. In vain were appeals made to the crowd to keep the peace and things went from bad to worse. Stones were thrown, blows were struck and the situation became really ugly. When the 'angels' were going to the fifth farm a large section of the crowd went to meet them and surrounded them. One man energetically beat a tin in the ears of Stephens, who was deafened by the noise. He rushed at the man's throat, and this led to others trying to strike Stephens. Free fighting now broke out, and the bailiffs and the police brought out their truncheons, which they used as best they could, cracking them on the craniums of those nearest at hand and having no regard for age or size. Their victims included children under fifteen, men over seventy, and women. Some were so severely injured that it was necessary to send Dr Pritchard, Denbigh, to attend to their wounds. One policeman and one bailiff were slightly injured. The Chief Constable read the Riot Act, and determined efforts were made to prevent the crowd renewing the attack. When the 'angels' returned to Denbigh they were greeted by worse hooting than had been the case in the morning, and but for the efforts of Mr Howell Gee there is no doubt that there would have been some more bloodshed, for the crowd was greatly excited.

The visit to Llannefydd was resumed on Friday with a strong retinue of 'angels' and police. Several farms were visited and in one place £2 was offered in pennies and half pennies. It is reported that one of the men is dying rapidly.

Report in *Y Genedl Cymreig* (May 23rd,1888)

Explosive Times
Stowers Johnson

Around Denbighshire there was not, as in South Wales, that early eighteenth-century flourishing of dissenters and 'secret' conventicles: indeed, there was violence towards the preachers, chapels were sometimes the target of mobs, and at least two (at Wrexham and Llanfyllin) were completely demolished. Around my little cottage there are four places in the hills which are still remembered as old centres of dancing and celebrations for holidays and feasting. For the preachers to sweep these away was something hard to take. But they did, though older folk can name these summer locations where fiddling and dancing were once surviving even on Sundays.

It was towards the end of the century that the stronger propaganda of Thomas Gee began to engender action across Denbighshire and strange it seems to us now, in this peaceful, God-fearing land, to read how the Reverend Venables of Conwy received a letter threatening, if he did not agree to reduction of the tithe, to blow up his vicarage with dynamite. Later, on 31 October 1886, the Mission Church, Colwyn Bay, was burned down.

from *Hearthstones in the Hills* (1987)

A Wartime Escape
Anon.

As we stood there in the gloaming, my companion told me that in August, 1915, one of the most daring escapes of the war was attempted from Dyffryn Aled [during the First World War this large country house was converted into a prisoner of war camp for captured German naval officers]. Three prisoners were involved. Together they made a careful investigation of the camp defences, and decided that, if a submarine could be sent to the north-west coast, escape was possible. Just then a fellow-prisoner was being sent back to Germany, through the exchange of prisoners arrangement, and through him they were able to send a message to the German naval authorities. In due course, the instructions for which they were waiting arrived, veiled in a letter which one of them received from Germany. On the appointed evening, they changed into civilian clothing, which they had concealed under the floor of their quarters, broke out, and soon were clear of the camp. Early the following morning they reached Llandudno, and making their way to the Great Orme, searched for suitable shelter. There they remained until nightfall, when they emerged to make their way to the beach below, but in the darkness they failed to find a way down. From the cliff top they made repeated flash lamp signals out to sea, but these remained unanswered. The next day they passed again in hiding, and that night, after making sure of the path before darkness fell, made their way to the beach without diffculty. They waited anxiously, but nothing happened. As time wore on, they made frantic signals out to sea, but again received no response. Having failed in their plans, their thoughts turned to other means of escape. They descended the Great Orme into Llandudno, but misfortune continued to dog their footsteps, and they were recognised and taken into custody. Afterwards it transpired that the submarine had been there all the time, but had come too far inshore, and had been hidden from view by a rocky headland. Thus ended what is believed to have been the only attempt by German war prisoners to escape from this country by submarine.

from *A Visitor's Impressions of Llansannan* (1922)

Casualties of Peace

Terence Doyle

THE GREAT WAR ended in 1918, but in 1919 soldiers in uniform were still being shot. At least Canadian soldiers were. Decorated veterans of the front lines, they were not to survive one last, unexpected battlefield — the gentle, green fields of North Wales. They were not to survive one last clash with a powerful enemy — their own commanding officers.

Six years ago independent film-maker Terry Ryan visited those same fields and heard for the first time in the surrounding hills an echo of this distant tragedy. Details were scant and facts conflicting. But there were people there who had actually been alive at the time and the same incongruous words recurred again and again. Canadian soldiers. Riots. Many deaths. Soldiers shot. In 1919.

'The day after this was first mentioned,' says Ryan 'I drove to the church of Bodelwyddan near Rhyl. It had been easy before then to doubt what I had heard. But the graves were there. The graves of eighty-three Canadians who had died, not in France or farther away during the war, but in Wales while they were going home.'

Ryan wanted to know how many had actually been shot. 'I wanted to know why any were shot at all. But the official sources were unforthcoming. In some cases the necessary information is classifed 'secret' and won't be made available until the next century. As well, there was confusion even at the time as to what actually happened.' What is known now is that in the second half of 1918 waves of Canadian soldiers from the front were sent to camps in north Wales to spend a week or two before sailing from Liverpool for home. The worst was behind them and the future in the form of family, friends and peace was all they thought of.

The camps were not what the triumphant victors might have expected. They could too easily seem only marginally better than a trench: cold, barren and crowded. But, unlike the trenches, they were temporary. The men knew their sailing dates, the hour when their war would be over forever.

Then the nightmare began. Instead of 'going home', they were crowded further by more soldiers. Where there had been reasonable room for one, there were now two, three, even four men. Summer died and winter raged fiercely. Suddenly influenza struck. Mates who had only weeks before cheered at having survived 'Fritz', now wasted away together.

And still no sailing dates were honoured. Instead there were rumours that they were not to return home after all but would go to Russia to fight again. Other said the ships had been diverted to carry goods instead of men.

In early March 1919 the situation somehow disintegrated. There were riots and soldiers were shot: Canadians had killed Canadians.

. . . Just a year ago, the coroner's reports on the dead men were released, establishing definitively that at least five did die from bullets — one was shot in the head — rather than from flu or fatigue. It also seems likely that the soldiers' suspicions about abuse in high office were true and the ships which never arrived were being diverted to carry grain from Canada to France and Germany. Even more provocative is evidence that survivors of the riots — veterans of battles which stir awe even today — were walked to their trials through the streets of Liverpool chained to each other.

On one of the gravestones in that Bodelwyddan churchyard, Ryan says, there was an epitaph: 'Some day, some time, we will understand'.

Radio Times (March 1987)

Stigmata
Tim Liardet

Kinmel Park Transit Camp, March. 1919

1

After France's mud for the dumped Canadians
The mud of Denbighshire, sucking at their puttees
And boots; just extricated, bulled for return.
Dock and home receded, flags and laden trams,
Such seedburst. While other trains got home
They were shunted out towards the dead-end
Of Ypres' depressing siding, the camp's half-world
Of the repetitious shedding of the moody rain
And remoteness of bleary coastal lights
To whose unheavenly promise one line led out.
After France's mud, delay, the back-end
Of a Welsh winter and the Quartermaster's nibs,
The thought of the great rainy Atlantic dividing.
Optical light. Occlusion. The submerged duck-boards
Bringing them back only to the commonplace
Of themselves, the smell of males in huts
Oppressed by their own animal repetitions,
Recycled breath and impotence to move at all,
Without heat, pay. 'The situation will be . . . ,'
etcetera. The daily evocations of army typewriters
Clacked against them, worse trenches than the trenches.
This was like the hoarse voice on the field-telephone —
Tapped though utterly dead — the voice which thinned
Until disembodied, receiving no answer.
Dampness seeped deeper, their blanketed heaps
Snaffled by influenza, booking the whole churchyard.

2
Too close to France's clouds, the undrained terrain
With every cloying boot-load of it symbolised
Beautiful gratitude. A prurient local culture
Compounded the wire, the limits contracting.
When the riot broke — flames seen from as far as Rhyl,
The shopkeepers of Abergele boarding up —
The British regiment was instructed, and sent in.
Five Canadians dead by cold light. Laid out
In the rain the human bodies seemed too slight
For such catharsis, punched through like buckets, as if
The bayonets had opened up more than flesh.
Stretcher-bearers resoiled their boots. The spokes
Of the field-ambulance picked up mud and slapped it back.

3
I'd seen wounds, but such as these — bayonet driving
The throat's muscles out through the back of the head —
Flesh burned to a charred star by close aiming —
Argued deeper resentment, something half understood,
As if to say these foreigners, being deprived,
Had brought too near a fancy for white breasts
Under buttons only we might undo, or failed
To scrape boots and begrimed an affected threshold
With too much unaffected ease, as if at home.
The British tried to trap the outcome in between
The trained sidling horse-flanks of official displacement,
Clopping up lanes, unspooling from their spurs
The godawful winter of the playful summer.

The constables pulled on their caps. After four years
Of foreign mud that never was quite brought in,
Of poachers in bicycle lamps, the comfort of dry socks,
The Constabulary was getting cocky again,
Brushing down its uniforms, ink in its pads,
Smelling the murders like pork after rationing.
Beyond the leather creaks of any doodling Court
The ditched Canadians were shunted out quick.
At Liverpool's dockside ensued a galvanic
Dumping of grain and design. Troopships became
Troopships again, the Coroner's inquest, well,

Postponed. The Canadians were blamed. The banshee
Of the truth fled from itself, finding protection.

Open-necked, unshaven, let no man mistake by whom
The five with mortuary-tags tied to their toes
Under the cloud cover of peacetime were used.
Pale translucence drawn to tendrils of smashed veins —
Ganglions of obscene intrusion, strained wrists —
Reproved the prophylaxis of British Lee-Enfields
Still waking the sweating minister forty years ahead.
Rainwater, waxed youth. We must assume something needed
Bayonet-holes through which to bleed. The victims
Were five in twelve million, drawn down after all
With Europe's ironmongery, a fivefold baring of heads
Of matted hair that could not be covered up
By five greatcoats, stained by such fresh springs of turmoil.

Tim Liardet's note on 'Stigmata':
The events of March 1919 at Kinmel Park Camp have remained something of an enigma for sixty years, in spite of their parochial notoriety.

The historiography of the riots is weak and there seems to be a reluctance in many quarters to speak openly about them. it is widely believed, however, that the Canadian soldiers, depressed and frustrated by incessantly postponed repatriation dates, squabbled amongst themselves, duly causing the deaths of five of their own number as a result and bullet- and bayonet-wounds.

In the monologue, an anonymous observer, possibily a doctor — drawn from the researchers and memories of various undisclosable sources — relates the events as he understands them.

from *Clay Hill* (1988)

The Gresford Disaster
Anon.

You've heard of the Gresford disaster,
Of the terrible price that was paid.
Two hundred and sixty-five colliers were lost,
And three men of a rescue brigade.

It occured in the month of September,
At three in the morning, that pit
Was wracked by a violent explosion
In the Dennis where gas lay so thick.

The gas in the Dennis deep section
Was heaped there like snow in a drift,
And many a man had to leave the coal-face
Before he had worked out his shift.

Now a fortnight before the explosion
To the shotfirer Tomlinson cried,
'If you fire that shot we'll be all blown to hell.'
And no one can say that he lied.

The fireman's reports they are missing,
The records of forty-two days:
The colliery manager had them destroyed
To cover his criminal ways.

Down in the dark they are lying,
They died for nine shillings a day.
They have worked out their shift and now they must lie
In the darkness until judgement day.
The Lord Mayor of London's collecting
To help out our children and wives,
The owners have sent some white lilies
To pay for the poor colliers' lives.

Farewell all our dear wives and children,
Farewell to our old comrades as well,
Saying, 'Don't send your sons down the dark dreary pit,
They'll be damned like the sinners in hell'.

A song written to commemorate the men killed in an explosion and fire at a colliery, near Wrexham in 1934.

The Grinding
I.D. Hooson

August 1940

Tumult in the ranks of the stars,
Strident, screeching, rending the night:
Eglwyseg, mountain aflame, and
Hell's hosts over Rhos in their might.

Hov'ring, burdened with woe as they
Roar furious, and loud overhead.
With the awful heat of their hate
The windows of high heaven are red.

Stupendous the hurling, and rush,
To its roots the village was shaken;
Stout buildings were felled, and their walls
Like leaves were scattered, and broken.

Strong men were bowed to the ground,
For shelter the boldest would fly,
In fear of the ceaseless bombardment,
The merciless bombing on high.

Are the gods then at work tonight?
Are the gods then grinding corn
Sown and reaped by man in the bread
Or sorrows for a world forlorn?

from *The Wine and other Poems*, trans. Blodwen Edwards (1984)

V E Day
Dewi Humphreys

May 8th — Tuesday VE-day
We had a holiday from school today in accordance with the national holiday because of our victory in Europe. It was the day for which we

had been waiting since September 1939 — five and a half years ago — five and a half years of the worst war in human history — so far.

There were hundreds of flags in Wrexham yesterday and hundreds of peace rumours. But, for once, the rumours were right — VE day was to be on the following day. Coedpoeth was full of flags — Mam had a big Union Jack hanging from her front window on a line-prop, but that did not affect our spirits. A length of bunting ran from our front window to one of [the] Cross Foxes windows, by mutual agreement, and in fact all the High Street was gay with flags. As coming up the hill from Wrexham one met three big flags hanging over the road — the British, Russian and American flags...

Although everyone was extremely happy, no one in our district went as mad as people did in 1918 after the other victory. People remained quite sane. There was hardly any drinking — not very much, at any rate; I expect it was because the beer was not plentiful, and when one could obtain it, it was pretty dear. There were no shoutings, processions, and people staying in the roads all night singing — nothing of that kind. Although the people were very happy, they controlled themselves, and many went to pray . . . .

In the twilight I could just see all the Rock, and saw hundreds of people standing on the football pitch there, and some standing on the rock overlooking the pitch. After some flares had been set off, the choir sang 'There'll always be an England'. Then some more flares, then we sang 'Rule Britannia' then more flares, and we sang a chorale, and then the last lot of flares. They went off with great reddish billows of smoke drifting over towards the village itself. So ended VE-day for me. I had a grand time, but, when I was in bed thinking of the past day, I could not help thinking of the thousands of lives taken away to give us such a happy and memorable day.

Ms. diary of Dewi Humphreys, Coedpoeth.

The Dornier

Gladys Mary Coles

The moorland blazing and a bomber's moon
lit skies light as a June dawn,
the harvest stubble to a guilty flush.

History

I saw from the farmhouse the smoking plane
like a giant bat in a sideways dive,
fuel spewing from its underbelly.
I remember how one wing tipped our trees
tearing the screen of pines like lace,
flipping over, flimsy as my balsa models.
It shattered on the pasture, killing sheep,
ripping the fence where the shot fox hung.
Dad let me look next morning at the wreck —
it lay in two halves like a broken wasp,
nose nestled in the ground, blades
of the propellers bent . . . .
I thought I saw them moving
in the wind.

If the Invader comes, the leaflet said,
Do not give a German anything. Do not tell him
anything. Hide your food and bicycles.
Hide your maps . . . . But these Luftwaffe men
were dead. Their machine, a carcass
cordoned off. A museum dinosaur.
Don't go nearer. Do not touch.

Trophies, I took — a section of the tail
(our collie found it dangling in the hedge),
pieces of perspex like thin ice on the grass,
some swapped for shrapnel down at school
(how strangely it burned in a slow green flame).
Inscribed *September 1940, Nantglyn,*
the black-crossed relic now hangs on our wall.
My son lifts it down, asks questions
I can't answer.

Yesterday, turning the far meadow for new drains,
our blades hit three marrows, huge and hard,
stuffed with High Explosive — the Dornier's final gift.
Cordoned off, they're photographed, defused.
I take my son to see the empty crater,
the imprint of their shapes still in the soil —
shadows that turn up time.

Nature Defeating Man

How easily nature defeats man and all his achievements — and an outstanding example of the power wielded by the elements was the manner in which last week's unexpected snowstorm threw the country into chaos. The blizzard began to 'blow up' late on Wednesday afternoon, sweeping snow on to roads and into every nook and cranny. As darkness descended, conditions worsened, and motorists in particular found themselves enveloped in a swirling, white world where landmarks were obscured and nothing looked the same as before. The blizzard raged all night, and morning light revealed a sorry state of affairs.

People in Denbighshire, after digging themselves out of their homes, found every road blocked by drifts which in some areas were up to thirteen feet in height. In fact for a time everything was at a standstill. That is, except for snow-ploughs and tractors which were tearing into the drifts, and re-opening up the county's lifelines. The rest we all know. Some semblance of order was restored through the efforts of the County Council staff and contractors brought in to help in the mammoth task. With some of the roads clear, residents of the rural areas were able to obtain the 'necessities' of life, but in some remote country areas, the weather dealt harshly with the residents, both human and animal, and for years to come, that March blizzard will be a talking point whenever hard weather is forecast.

Denbighshire Free Press (March 1965)

The Men Who Make the Steel

Ian Chesterman

Chorus

To take away the right to earn a decent living wage,
The furnaces they'll soon be closing down;
The sky no more will glow and six thousand jobs must go
For the men who make the steel in Shotton Town.

The man who came along one day, he told them they would have
to pay —
The price of progress now it seems is high;

For the British Steel Committee sat in judgement in the city
And produced a piece of paper that can't lie.

It seems that they are out of date, in 1975 the fate
Of many working men will be resolved;
For like the men who work the coal they too will soon be on the dole
And looking round the country for a job.
Lord Melchett's just like me and you, at nine o'clock he turns to view
The very latest news on his TV;
He sees the steelmen march along, but does he really know what's wrong,
And can he really see what they can see?

The steelmen know their cause is right, they won't give up without a fight,
Until the very last day comes along;
They're fighting for a living and you know that they won't give in
Until they prove that piece of paper wrong.

These are the words of a song written to popularize the cause for retaining steel-making at Shotton. It was issued on a 45 r.p.m. record in 1975.

Misrule, Towyn, 1990
Steve Griffiths

With a clatter, the sea pushes
its tongue through the letterbox.
It does not empty or relieve itself.
The Axminster rises towards the ceiling,
passing a barometer half way up.

This is my home and I'm having it back
from the sea: swilling up to the front room sill
and window-frame, newly reglossed
in duck-egg blue,
fourteen years of marriage.
Grateful to find there are knickers

intact on the top shelf: one pair fresh
as rising dough on the hearth
and I'm ready to meet my maker.

Hers is a small house
in a silent gallery of snow,
in a plastic capsule won from a cracker,
broken soon: a hermit crab
darts below the swirling fall of sand
among the surging levities of beach-plastic
and the shoes that feel life returning
in the bedroom.
The rattle of shingle
is uniform and triumphant
across the kitchen floors of Towyn.

On a roof anchored uncertainly with planks,
there were ovals of grey ice
on blue plastic sheeting
like lakes from a plane in blue mountains
as I lean down from an early meal.

Over his muesli, my son asks
if it was like this in Atlantis,
a little water
riding together suddenly
over the flat of his hand
as he lowers it in the bath,
knocking the houses over, like this.

I must have been twelve or thereabouts
when I pored through the atlas,
speculating what would be left of the uplands

if the sea reached six hundred feet,
recording it all meticulously
as the sea blustered
not far from the door:

the West Siberian Plain,
the basin of the Ganges and the Brahmaputra,

History

the Fens, the North European Plain,
most of Cheshire
was it the fury of clouds I wanted
or simply disorder,
was it a sad end,
was it a just desert
or the little death
that sets a story in motion?
The strong winds rage along the isobars
and people begin not to notice
how it plucks and tears at awnings,
raging at bars,
perhaps more than it did before.
On the way to work,
I noticed how the buildings
loitered in the street,
how I could have stopped
and watched anything happen:

it was a sharp cold day,
people ran to the river bank
as a shack approached
and floated slowly past:
at the open back a boy and a small girl,
between them a dog with its back to the water,
the boy taking pulls of a cigarette,
the girl holding the tip of the dog's tail
between her fingers in the same way,
pale and very concentrated.
We were left gawping.

We felt our ways
upstream and down
for something familiar.

But now you cannot retreat as far as the sea
you belong to
because it will come for you.

from *Selected Poems* (1993)

Culture and Religion

At the Eisteddfod

Dylan Thomas

Llangollen. A town in a vale in rolling green North Wales on a windy July morning. The sun squints out and is puffed back again into the grey clouds blowing, full to the ragged rims with rain, across the Berwyn Hills. The white-horsed River Dee hisses and paws over the hills of its stones and under the greybeard bridge. Wind smacks the river and you, it's a cold, cracking morning; birds hang and rasp over the whipped river, against their will, as though frozen still, or are wind-chaffed and scattered towards the gusty trees. As you drift down Castle Street with your hair flying, or your hat or umbrella dancing to be off and take the sky, you see and hear all about you the decorous, soberly dressed and headgeared, silent and unsmiling inhabitants of the tame town. You could be in any Welsh town on any windy snip of a morning, with only the birds and the river fuming and the only brightness the numberless greens and high purples of the hills. Everything is very ordinary in Llangollen; everything is nicely dull, except the summer world of wind and feathers, leaves and water. There is, if you are deaf, blind, and dumb, with a heart like cold bread pudding, nothing to remark or surprise. But rub your eyes with your black gloves. Here, over the bridge, come three Javanese, winged, breastplated, helmeted, carrying gongs and steel bubbles. Kilted, sporraned, tartan'd, daggered Scotsmen reel and strath-spey up a side-street, piping hot. Burgundian girls, wearing, on their heads, bird-cages made of velvet suddenly whisk on the pavement into a coloured dance. A viking goes into a pub. In black felt feathered hats and short leather trousers, enormous Austrians, with thighs big as Welshmen's bodies, but much browner, yodel to fiddles and split the rain with their smiles. Frilled, ribboned, sashed, fezzed, and white-turbaned, in baggy-blue sharavári and squashed red boots, Ukrainians with Manchester accents gopak up the hill. Everything is strange in Llangollen. You wish you had a scarlet hat, and bangles, and a little bagpipe to call your own, but it does not matter. The slapping bell-dancers, the shepherds and chamois-hunters, the fiddlers and fluters, the players on gongs and mandolines, guitars, harps, and trumpets, the beautiful flashing boys and girls of a score and more of singing countries, all the colours of the international rainbow, do not mind at all your mouse-brown moving among them: though you long, all the long Eisteddfod week, for a cloak like a blue sea or a bonfire to sweep and blaze in the wind, and a cap of bells, and a revelling waistcoat, and a great Alp-horn to blow all over Wales from the ruins of Dinas Brân.

Now follow your nose, and the noise of guitars, and the flying hues and flourish of those big singing-birds in their clogs and aprons and bonnets, veils, flowers, more flowers, and lace, past the wee Shoppes, the rough the babel of the bridge, by the very white policeman conducting from a rostrum, and up the tide of the hill, past popcorn and raspberryade, to the tented Field.

Green, packed banks run, swarming, down to the huge marquee there that groans and strains and sings in the sudden squalls like an airship crewed full of choirs. Music spills out of the microphones all over the humming field. Out of the wind-tugged tent it rises in one voice and the crowd outside is hushed away into Spain. In a far corner of the field, young men and women begin to dance, for every reason in the world. Out skims the sun from a cloud-shoal. The spaniel ears of the little tents flap. Children collect the autographs of Dutch farmers. You hear a hive of summer hornets: it is the Burgundian *vielle*, a mandolin with a handle. Palestrina praises from Bologna to the choral picnickers. A Breton holiday sings in the wind, to clog-tramp and *biniou*.

Here they come, to this cup and echo of hills, people who love to make music, from France, Ireland, Norway, Italy, Switzerland, Spain, Java, and Wales: fine singers and faulty, nimble dancers and rusty, pipers to make the dead swirl or chanters with crows in their throats: all countries, shapes, ages, and colours, sword-dancers, court-dancers, cross-dancers, clog-dancers, dale-dancers, morris, ceilidhe, and highland, bolero, flamenco, heel-and-toe. They love to make music move. What a rush of dancing to Llangollen's feet! And, oh, the hubbub of tongues and toes in the dark chapels where every morning there's such a shining noise as you'd think would drive the Sunday bogles out of their doldrums for ever and ever.

from Quite Early One Morning (1954)

A Village of Colliers
Raymond Edwards

My village of colliers [Rhosllanerchrugog] turned out few poets, one only of real distinction, surprisingly few creative people, but a whole regiment of teachers and preachers, lecturers, professors, vice-chancellors and college principals, without whom the Principality would, I imagine, have been much the poorer.

from *Artists in Wales*, edited by Meic Stephens (1973)

What Passes and Endures
John Ceiriog Hughes

Still do the great mountains stay,
    And the winds above them roar;
There is heard at break of day
    Songs of shepherds as before.
Daisies as before yet grow
    Round the foot of hill and rock;
Over these old mountains, though,
    A new shepherd drives his flock.

To the customs of old Wales
    Changes come from year to year;
Every generation fails,
    One has gone, the next is here.
After a lifetime tempest-tossed
    Alun Mabon is no more,
But the language is not lost
    And the old songs yet endure.

trans. Tony Conran

The Caerwys Eisteddfod
Gwyn Williams

There was trouble in the world of poetry, trouble which reflected the changes in the social order in Wales. Not all the new gentry were prepared to employ a house poet or to welcome an itinerant one, and, to make matters worse, unqualified poets were wandering about the country and putting the trained bards out of business. Elizabeth issued an order to some gentlemen of North Wales that they should hold an eisteddfod at Caerwys to set matters right. It went thus:

> Elizabeth by the Grace of God, of England, France and Ireland; Queen, and Defender of the Faith . . . to our trusty and right well beloved Sir Richard Bulkely, Knight; Ellis Price, Doctor in Civil Law and one of our Council in the Marches of Wales; William Mostyn . . . and to every of them greeting. Whereas it is come to the knowledge of the Lord President and other our council in the Marches of Wales that vagrant and idle persons, naming themselves Minstrels, Rythmers and Bards, are lately grown into such intolerable multitude within the Principality of North Wales, that not only gentlemen and others are often disquieted in their habitations but also the expert minstrels and musicians . . . much discouraged in the Practice of their know ledge, and also not a little hindered of livings and preferment; the reformation thereof and putting these people in order, the said Lord President and Council have thought very necessary . . . Our said Council have therefore appointed the execution of this commission to be at the town of Caerwys, the Monday next after the Feast of the Blessed Trinity, which shall be in the year of our Lord, 1568. And, therefore, to require and command you, by the authority of these presents, to cause open proclamation to be made that all and every person and persons that intend to maintain their living by name or colour of Minstrels, Rythmers and Bards appear before you, the said day and place to show their Leanings accordingly . . . .
>
> Also that you Sir Richard Bulkeley, Ellis Price and William Mostyn, Esquires, repair to the place the day aforesaid . . . to admit such as by your wisdom and knowledges you shall find worthy to use, exercise and follow the Sciences and Faculties of their Professions . . . giving straight-monition and commendment in our name to the rest not worthy, that they return to some honest labour . . . upon pain to be taken as sturdy and

> idle vagabonds . . . . Given under our signet at our City of Chester the 23rd of October, in the ninth year of our reign, 1567.

Elis Prys, the Ellis Price of this document, was known as *Y Doctor Coch*, the Red Doctor, because of his Cambridge gown, and was one of the most feared men in North Wales. He had been one of Henry VIII's 'visitors' for the dissolution of the monasteries and was a ruthless land-grabber, both for himself and his great friend, Robert Dudley, Earl of Leicester. He was the father of Thomas Prys, Plas Iolyn, the pirate poet. The Mostyn family had long been notable patrons of poetry and the queen's commission reminded William Mostyn that 'his ancestors have had the gift and bestowing of the silver harp appertaining to the Chief of that faculty'. On this occasion the silver harp went to Simwnt Fychan, a scholarly poet who did much to carry on the traditions of the classical Welsh metres and who must often have recited his verse to the company in the noble hall which William Mostyn built and which today stands at a higher level than the bigger and more splendid Mostyn Hall.

Caerwys is today a sleepy little place and unlikely as a setting for a National Eisteddfod, which today depends on the common people of Wales for support, not on its gentry.

from *The Land Remembers* (1977)

Hugh Holland

A.S. Vaughan Thomas

'The iniquity of oblivion,' says Sir Thomas Browne in his *Hydrotaphia*, 'blindly scattereth his poppy, and deals with the memory of man without distinction to merit of perpetuity.' Time is often an arbitrary, but rarely a casual critic, and those writers whose fame has not survived the approval of their own generation can usually be shown to deserve their fate.

Not even the natural enthusiasm of the biographer can promote the reputation of Hugh Holland higher than it stands today. He is chiefly remembered for his verses prefixed to the first folio of Shakespeare, and the talent there revealed does not encourage any critic to consider other work of his worth reprinting.

Yet he was a man of considerable reputation in his day and if he must be condemned by the very highest standards of judgement, his life and work are nevertheless worthy of attention. No man whose interest in the arts was as catholic as Holland's is without value to posterity. The study of his career, ambitions and achievements becomes a social document of some importance. The man who was taught his Latin by the great Camden, who toured the continent in the style of a man of means; who came back to London to be the friend of Ben Jonson and take his place among the wits of the Mermaid Tavern; who was mentioned with interest by Spenser and Sidney, and himself found favour at court; who was called by his old schoolmaster 'one of the most pregnant wits of those times' and knew writers like Sir Thomas Hawkins, and musicians like William Byrde, Dr. John Bull and Orlando Gibbons, was clearly a person of wide and cultured contacts. An enquiry into his career, therefore is not a piece of literary futility, merely because it cannot honestly raise his reputation. Hugh Holland is best remembered not so much as a poet but as a cultured man, who enjoyed the society of others more gifted than himself.

from *Hugh Holland* (1943)

Artists in Clwyd

Donald Moore

Some of these travellers were of local origin, but many came from the direction of England. For most, the ultimate goal was the craggy height of Snowdon, so they moved westwards, normally on foot, perhaps assisted by horses, and occasionally in a carriage (provided the road was suitable). To reach Snowdon they were obliged to pass through the north-east corner of Wales, then represented by two counties, Flintshire and Denbighshire. Although the Clwydian hills were not spectacular enough to elicit great admiration, there was much in the area to detain them in buildings that witnessed man's handiwork over the centuries.

The proximity of Clwyd to the English border has always made it accessible to new influences from the east, and these are evident in fine architecture. The local nobility and gentry took a proprietorial interest in their surroundings and their history. Most had had their vision sharpened on the Grand Tour of the Continent, and they saw new delights in their own acres as a result. In 1771 the great landowner, Sir Watkin Williams Wynn of Wynnstay, near Ruabon, paid a well-known landscape artist, Paul Sandby, to accompany him in a coach on a picturesque tour of north Wales; Sandby, Chief Drawing Master at Woolwich Military Academy, gave his patron the benefit of tuition. He also published a set of twelve aquatint prints, based on the sketches which he had made during the tour.

A lesser landowner, Thomas Pennant of Downing in Flintshire (1726-98), employed a full-time artist, Moses Griffith, to produce illustrations for his numerous publications. Pennant is remembered today mainly as an antiquarian writer, but in his own time he was renowned as a zoologist, botanist and geologist. Moses Griffith was born in humble circumstances in Llŷn. Apparently without formal training, he became a skilful watercolourist. His works have a 'primitive' quality as have those of another of Pennant's illustrators, John Ingleby of Flint.

These are examples of collaboration between patron and artist in the late eighteenth century, when artistic interest in the north Wales landscape reached a climax. How did the story begin? We look in vain in Wales for the prolific output of art which characterised the Netherlands in the seventeenth century. Apart from portraits of the gentry, hardly any pictures were produced. The work of one seventeenth century artist figures in this exhibition, albeit as a print published a hundred years later; this is St. Winifred's Well by Francis Place. Castles were the most impressive man-made structures in the landscape; they were the symbols of the power and authority of the ruling class (whether that had been Welsh or English). Clwyd had two massive castles built by Edward I, at Flint and Rhuddlan, as well as many earlier strongholds. Comparably large buildings were monasteries, in ruins as a result of the Reformation, but still exciting wonder at the skill of their construction; the overtones of a vanished religion heightened this feeling. There had been monasteries in Clwyd at Basingwerk, Rhuddlan, Denbigh, Ruthin and Valle Crucis, but the best known and most visited was the last. A short detour from the Holyhead road brought the traveller into a picturesque valley — the Vale of Cross — where the Cistercians had chosen a rural retreat in the thirteenth century; the Cross of the Vale was there: a monument erected in the ninth century to commemorate a Welsh king of Powys.

Clwyd had one cathedral, St. Asaph, small and plain, and surrounded by a mere village, but important as the seat of spiritual power. Throughout the area were parish churches of great architectural interest and antiquity. These were destinations for the artists. A site of architectural, antiquarian and religious interest which had survived the Reformation was Saint Winifred's Well at Holywell. Still a centre of pilgrimage, it was a constant subject for artists from the seventeenth century onwards.

from *The Artist's Journey Through North Wales: Clwyd* (1991)

An After Dinner Discourse
Samuel Johnson

I dined at Mr Myddleton's, of Gwaenynog . . . . After dinner, the talk was of preserving the Welsh language. I offered them a scheme. Poor Evan Evans was mentioned as incorrigibly addicted to strong drink. Washington was commended. Myddleton is the only man who, in Wales, has talked to me of literature. I wish he were truly zealous. I recommended the republication of David ap Rhees's Welsh Grammar.

from *A Diary of a Journey through North Wales* (1774)

Gaining Cheap Admittance
Cecil Price

Thomas Jones of Denbigh declares that a band of actors came to the town 'about 1771' and, since they could not get a place to suit them, asked a carpenter to erect a temporary wooden theatre. This was built in a garden and the boys of the town planned to dig a small hole under the wooden wall and gain a cheap admittance. Thomas Jones describes how, with his accomplices, he scraped away the soft earth and wriggled into the theatre. As soon as they were inside, they realized that they would see nothing of the play because the tiered seats were above and in front of them. They found a gap however, and were aided by a few kind friends who dragged them into the auditorium. To these helpers they owed their lives for, a minute later, the rickety structure collapsed and people and forms were thrown into the dark space which the boys had just quitted.

from *The English Theatre in Wales*, 1948.

A Theatre-goer with a Cloven Hoof
A. H. Dodd

During the second half of the eighteenth century the theatrical performances given at Sir Watkins Williams Wynn's private theatre at Wynnstay were great occasions. Members of the county families, old and young, from the Wrexham neighbourhood, and from all over the county, took part in these productions. Tickets for the performances were in great demand, and a writer of the time says that the gatherings 'gave a character to the neighbourhood'. The baronet was a patron of literature and the arts, and was well acquainted with the leading figures of the time. He kept open house for several weeks in winter, with several performances taking place each week. Many distinguished visitors came to Wynnstay on these occasions, including Garrick, Sheridan, and Maddocks of Tremadoc fame. In the Wynnstay accounts, under January 6, 1771, there is a reference to a sum of £8 9s. 0d. paid to the Wrexham players for playing at Wynnstay . . . .

An Act of 1843 made it easier for players in the provinces by removing restrictions, but meanwhile standards of propriety were changing; and although the gentry patronised the playhouses, their example did not count as much as formerly in the community. Some people kept away from the theatre for the sake of their reputation. We must also not forget the attitude of some of the religious leaders to stage plays; they were uncompromising in their opposition. John Elias had prohibited the playing of interludes in Anglesey in 1802, and the disciplinary rules of the Calvanistic Methodists condemn *chwaraeyddiaethau*, a term which certainly includes stage plays. This opposition may have had something to do with the persistence of the legend that upon a certain Saturday night in the Wynnstay theatre a gentleman dressed in black, with a cloven hoof, made an unexpected appearance on the stage, and that the theatre had not been opened since.

from *A History of Wrexham* (1957)

Theatr Clwyd
T.M. Haydn Rees

Her Majesty The Queen, accompanied by H.R.H. The Duke of Edinburgh, officially opened Theatr Clwyd Arts Centre and the Educational Technology Centre on a beautiful afternoon on 21 May 1976, and there were tremendous crowds to greet our Royal Visitors. During the afternoon ceremony, the Clwyd Youth Orchestra under their Conductor Roland Morris and a party of young school harpists under Ceinwen Steward took part. In the evening, we had Wales' first Royal Gala Performance with the BBC Welsh Symphony Orchestra, Emlyn Williams and Elizabeth Vaughan. It was a joyous end to a marvellous day.

The Theatre gained a national reputation. London's foremost critics were soon coming to the Theatre. *The Sunday Times* critic was soon writing 'Theatre Clwyd in Mold: what an amazing place! Imagine a town of fewer than 9,000 inhabitants with a well equipped and many purposed building erected by some miracle of regional generosity and enterprise . . . . One might have been in Germany'. The *Observer* critic has described it as 'the best appointed and most astonishing of the maisons de culture . . .'. *The Times* called it 'a splendidly equipped Theatre'. Just before the opening of the Theatre, the then Minister of the Arts, Mr. Hugh Jenkins after a tour of the building said 'The whole complex is the physical answer to the gloom of the despairmongers; it is superb and worthy of its site and the people responsible for this are looking to a future in which young people will be able to live and work and even lead a fuller life. I have always taken the view that the arts are properly seen as an extension and perhaps the ultimate purpose of education'. And there are countless others who have made similar observations.

May I wish the Theatre well in the future.

from *Theatr Clwyd: 1976-1986.*

Richard Wilson

David Bell

He was clearly a keenly intelligent man interested in the world about him, witty in conversation, and a good companion. But, like many painters, he appears to have been more tolerant of other people's opinions when they did not concern art. He did not suffer fools gladly. In particular he did not care much for the connoisseur or self-styled expert in art, but was warm in friendship to his fellow painters and his pupils, as his list of apprentices and students would indicate. He would seem to have carried his success well. His appearance as a young man may be gauged from the portrait which a fellow artist, Raphael Mengs (1728-79), painted of him in Rome and which is now in the National Museum of Wales. It shows a pleasant, open, but not particularly handsome face, which a rather bulbous nose does not improve, a nose which in his decline and under the influence of claret became almost grotesque and was rudely commented on by his contemporaries. In the days of his success Wilson was a pleasant, intelligent fellow.

As taste changed he found it increasingly difficult to sell the pictures he painted or to find people who would commission them. He became poor, and — as so often happens when fortune in life takes that turn — he became short-tempered and bitter against the world. This is the man about whom most of the stories are told and who is most often remembered. In the days of his success Wilson had been one of the founder-members of the Royal Academy, which was founded in 1768, and now in 1776 when his fortunes were in a decline his friends found him employment as the Academy's librarian. He held this post until his health failed him, when he left London to return to Wales. However, he continued to paint until the year before his death, and exhibited pictures in the new Royal Academy almost every year until 1780. He died in Denbighshire in 1782, and was buried in the churchyard at Mold, in Flintshire.

from *The Artist in Wales*, 1957.

Dreadful, Vulgar, Out-of-tune Trash...
Felix Mendelssohn

Ten thousand devils take all national music! Here I am in Wales, and, heaven help us! a harper sits in the hall of every reputable tavern playing so called folk melodies — that is to say, dreadful, vulgar, out-of tune trash with a hurdy-gurdy going on at the same time!

It has given me toothache already. Anyone who, like myself, can't stand Beethoven's national songs ought to come to Wales and hear them bellowed by rough nasal voices to the crudest accompaniment — and then try to keep his temper. As I write a fellow in the hall is playing . . . it makes me so angry I can't go on.

in a letter from an inn at Llangollen (1829)

The Musical 'Boots'
Michael Faraday

We had time this morning to enjoy the inn we had entered and which possesses a very high character of cleanliness, attention and comfort. We certainly found it so . . . . Whilst at breakfast, the River Dee flowing before our windows, the second harper I have heard in Wales struck his instrument and played some airs in very excellent style. I enjoyed them for a long time and then, wishing to gratify myself with the sight of the interesting bard, went to the door and behold — the boots! He, on seeing me open the door, imagined I wanted something and quitting his instrument took up his third character of waiter. I must confess I was sadly disappointed and extremely baulked. Even at Bethgellert they had a good looking blind old man though he played badly and now when I heard delightful sounds and had assured myself the Harper was in accordance with the effect he produced, he sank on a sudden many many stages down into a common waiter. Well: After all I certainly left Llangollen regretting the harp less than the person who played it.

Journal of a Tour Through Wales, (1819)

Music in the Cathedral

Raymond Renowden

Some words of Joanna Trollope from her novel, *The Choir*, come to me. She is describing the scene in the Cathedral before the Organ Appeal service begins. Mr. Beckford, a highly gifted musician and assistant organist, is playing a work by Bach and she writes:

> The faces all down the nave, row upon row, were reflecting whether their owners meant them or not, the effects of the building, the music and the occasion, all at once full of power and excitement and peace.

How apposite these words are for the many concerts and recitals given in this remarkable building. They take us beyond the ideas of mere co-operation and practical utility to a more treasured koinonia.

As we reflect on the role of the Cathedral in this, there are two elements to ponder. Certainly, there is the building itself, widely famed for its acoustic qualities. A mixture of architecture dating from the thirteenth to the nineteenth centuries, it has a certain unity and harmony and sound in the Cathedral has a definite purity of texture whether from an oboe or guitar, piano or violin, a human voice or a grand orchestra. Professor William Mathias [first artistic director of the music festival] never ceased to speak proudly of this and it underlined his conviction that St. Asaph Cathedral was the only place for the North Wales Music Festival. The great artists who have come here over the years have paid tribute to this element. One said to me, 'this cathedral must be one of the finest concert-halls in Europe'.

The secret of the Cathedral is the paradox of sound and silence, the silence which is not just the absence of sound but a creative impulse beyond complete analysis or description and yet, is enriching and nourishing.

from *Cathedral and Festival: A Partnership in Music*, the printed text of the 1993 annual festival lecture

A Scholar's Early Home

Robert Roberts

From a literary point of view there was not much to be seen. Two or three broadsides, adorned with woodcuts, hideous no doubt, but in our estimation, creditable specimens of the pictorial art, were pasted on various parts of the white-washed walls. One is a doleful ditty about the great storm of 1839, detailing in unmelodious numbers the damages done to ships and buildings by that calamity over the letterpress is a woodcut of Menai Bridge, coloured green, surprinted by a bright yellow ship in full sail. Another is a song of 'meditations' on a clock striking, aptly embellished by a picture of an eight-day clock, surrounded by various nondescript figures. A third is a ballad about the Chartist riots at Newport adorned with a wonderful picture of a skirmish in a wood apparently and not in the streets; but this slight departure from fact was of no moment and the illustration was thought to be a great success. Two or three small engravings of wonderfully ill-favoured non-conformist divines make up the list of pictorial illustrations.

In one or two short shelves near the great pewter-adorned dresser rests the humble stock of books which, scanty as it is, is larger than is usually found in Welsh farmhouses in the days of my youth, whatever may be the case now. Conspicuous among them is a large folio Bible, with Peter Williams's commentary. This is the family Bible, where the births, deaths, and marriages are entered. This is the great Hall Bible, always used at family prayers, and it was out of this that I learned my first letter.

The taste of the readers is easily seen from the fact of most of the books being theological. Among the older sort are *The Whole Duty of Man*, the *History of the Faith*, *The Pilgrim's Progress*, and the *Welshman's Candle*, or the *Vicar's Book*, a great favourite with old-fashioned Welshmen to this day. This book, next to the Bible, was my earliest reading book. I read and re-read its homely rugged rhymes till I could repeat the greater part off by heart. It was my great-grand-mother's constant companion. In spite of her great age she could read large print without glasses, and the *Vicar's Book* was seldom out of her hands, except when she was knitting. My first quarrel with the old lady was about taking possession of her book. Among the newer are two commentaries, half a dozen volumes of polemical tracts, and the works of Gurnal, a work very popular in Wales. Of profane literature there is very little: the *Mirror of the Primitive Age* and *Afternoon of Wales* furnish all the history, and *Roberts's Geography*, a good book, written on the plan of Guthrie's *Geographical Grammar*, supplies all the geography; a few poems, those of Goronwy Owen, Lewis Morris, Hugh Morris, and some of Twm o'r Nant's *Interludes*, or religious plays as he calls them, served for *belles lettres*. There were no English books, all were Welsh save an old battered Adam Lyttleton's Latin dictionary, a relic of the more varied taste, or education of some member of the family in remote times. There were no newspapers, for there was none published in that part of Wales at that time, but there were two monthly periodicals, *Y Drysorfa* (a Methodist magazine), and *Y Gwladgarwr*, a secular paper something like the old *Penny Magazine*.

from *A Wandering Scholar*, 1923.

Ferocious Honesty

Derek Llwyd Morgan

She has strived unstintingly to promote the cause of Welsh Nationalism in Denbigh and here in Wales. Her ferocious honesty has made her a fearsome figure; but again those who know her know her wit and humour and hearty laughter. In retirement, she took her place in the van of those who petitioned and worked for a Welsh-medium primary school in Denbigh, and Ysgol Twm o'r Nant is as much a monument to her spirit as it is a memorial to the eighteenth-century playwright. Like Annie's in 'Dychwelyd' her house is at the end of a private lane. I know that she has often been pestered there by trespassing schoolboys, who seem to cultivate as a sport the vexing of old disciplinarians, whose principles and belief — Kate Roberts's are at once conservative and revolutionary — no doubt appear to them totally eccentric.

from *Kate Roberts* (1974)

Reflections
Kate Roberts

I am old — if I can live a few months longer I will have reached the promised age. I sit by the fire reflecting on what I have written, and thinking how much of music there is in it. I've been in Denbigh for a quarter of a century, living in a town where I don't hear very much Welsh: what there is here is poor Welsh, even in the chapel. The standard of public speaking is low here. Across the years from what I have written come the voices of people who could speak publicly in sumptuous Welsh, who could pray in a refined vocabulary, 'Cymer ni i Dy nawdd ac i'th amddiffyn sylw. Rhagora ar ein dymuniadau gwael ac annheilwng (Take us to Thy refuge and to Thy safeguarding notice. Surpass our base and unworthy desires)'.

from *The World of Kate Roberts* (1991) trans. Joseph Clancy

Struggle
Kate Roberts

With us everything is a struggle. In my own case the fight of which I am most proud was the establishment of a Welsh Primary School, Ysgol Twm o'r Nant, in Denbigh in 1968. You may say we should not have to fight and struggle for things that should be ours by right. On the other hand it is no bad thing to struggle. As much as our writing it provides that tension which prolongs the life of a culture and presents from one day to another the possibility of fresh insights into the true nature of the human condition.

from *The Triple Net*, ed. Emyr Humphreys, 1990.

Bits and Pieces
Euros Bowen

We must glean the fields in the world as it is, for bits and pieces gather everywhere, tinder of the wind and the rain in the river mouth, worthless little twigs on the lawn, fragments of cobweb in the wasting away of autumn, heaps of leaves at the bottoms of ditches, old circulars, committee reports, clichés of devotion and creed in the mind's attic, dust, debris and ashbins, overspill of peevish smoke on chimneys, and rusty old tins in the river bed.

Why talk of stray bits and pieces like these, and bother to note them? — odds-and-ends of observation that matter to no one and nothing...

A man came by with a lorry today, collecting old iron to be cast into Brymbo's furnaces...

Why talk of bits and pieces?

—Because the scrap melts to a message in the poem.

from *Twentieth Century Welsh Poems*, trans. Joseph Clancy.

Llanrhaeadr-ym-Mochnant

R.S. Thomas

This is where he sought God.
And found him? The centuries
Have been content to follow
Down passages of serene prose.

There is no portrait of him
But in the gallery of
The imagination: a brow
With the hair's feathers
Spilled on it; a cheek
Too hollow; rows of teeth
Broken on the unmanageable bone
Of language; in this small room
By the river expiating the sin
Of his namesake.
The smooth words
Over which his mind flowed
Have become an heirloom. Beauty

Is how you say it, and the truth,
Like this mountain-born torrent,
Is content to hurry
Not too furiously by.

from *Not That He Brought Flowers* (1968)

St. Winefride's Well

Gerard Manley Hopkins

After Winefride's raising from the dead and the breaking out of the fountain.

Oh now while skies are blue, now while seas are salt
  While rushy rains shall fall or brooks shall fleet from fountains,
While sick men shall cast sighs, of sweet health all despairing,
  While blind men's eyes shall thirst after daylight, draughts of daylight
Or deaf ears shall desire that lipmusic that's lost upon them,
While cripples are, while lepers, dancers in dismal limb dance,
    Fallers in dreadful frothpits, waterfearers wild,
Stone, palsy, cancer, cough, lung-wasting, womb not bearing
    Rupture, running sores, what more? In brief, in burden,
As long as men are mortal and God merciful,
    So long to this sweet spot, this leafy lean-over,
This dry dene, now no longer dry nor dumb, but moist and musical
With the uproll and the downcarol of day and night delivering
Water, which keeps thy name, (for not in rock written,
But in pale water, frail water, wild rash and reeling water,
That will not wear a print, that will not stain a pen,
Thy venerable record, virgin, is recorded)
Here to this holy well shall pilgrimages be,
And not from purple Wales only nor from elmy England,
But from beyond seas, Erin, France and Flanders every where,
Pilgrims, still pilgrims, more pilgrims, still more poor pilgrims.
What sights shall be when some that swung, wretches, on crutches
Their crutches shall cast from them, on heels of air departing,
Or they go rich as roseleaves hence that loathsome came hither!
Not now to name even

Those dearer, more divine boons whose haven the heart is.
As sure as what is most sure, sure as that spring
primroses shall new-dapple next year, sure as to-morrow
morning, amongst come-back-again things, things with
a revival, things with a recovery.
Thy name [*Winefride will live*]. . . .

Blind Zeale

Celia Fiennes

. . . It seems the Saint they do honour to in this place must beare them out in all things, they tell of many lameness's and aches and distempers which are cured by it; its a cold water and cleare and runs off very quick so that it would be pleasant refreshment in the summer to washe onesself in it, but its shallow not up to the waist so its not easy to dive and washe in . . . . I saw abundance of the devout papists on their knees all round the wall; poor people are deluded into an ignorant blind zeale and to be pity'd by us that have the advantage of knowing better and ought to be better; there is some small stones of a reddish coullour in the well said to be some of St. Winifred's blood also, which the poor people take out and bring to the strangers for curiousity and relicts, and also moss about the bancks full of great virtue for every thing — but its a certain game to the poore people, every one gives them something for bringing them moss and the stones . . .

from *Through England on a Side Saddle in the Time of William and Mary* (1698)

A Complete and Miraculous Cure'

Philip Metcalf, S.J.

WARDOUR, 3 *Dec.*, 1830.
REV. AND DEAR SIR, — I have delayed too long to inform you that the person in whose behalf I wrote to you some time ago for some of the moss and the water of St. Winefride's Well, has by the blessing of

God, obtained a complete and miraculous cure of her maladies. The name of the person cured, I think I told you, is Mary White. She is one of my congregation and a convert to our holy religion. Her complaint, as I informed you, was a cancer in the face, under which she had long been suffering, and for the cure of which she had been admitted into the Salisbury infirmary, and had there been pronounced by the best medical attendants as a case *incurable*.

Other discharge from the infirmary, her surgeon, the eminent surgeon, Dr. Wates, of Salisbury, certified that the cartilage of one side of her nostril was eaten through by the cancer, so as to render a surgical operation impracticable; the whole of her face, especially the nose and inside of her mouth, were greatly affected, so that no hopes were entertained of any medical aid.

At the recommendation of Lord and Lady Arundell, I applied to you for some of the moss and water of St. Winefride's Well. On receiving the parcel you had the goodness to send, we explained to the patient that she was not to consider the application as any charm or medical remedy, but to be used and applied in the prayer of faith, confiding in the goodness of God and the powerful intercession of His saints. On the first application the patient declared she found the pains which she had so long suffered ceased. She continued to use the application of the moss and water for a considerable time (as long, indeed, as any of the moss and water remained). The dreadful wound gradually healed, and now I am happy to inform you that the cancer is perfectly cured. Thanks be to God and to the intercession of His holy Saint!

Moreover, I wish to inform you that she had lost the use of her sight in her right eye for the space of about thirteen years. This may perhaps have proceeded from the same malady. But I desired her to make at the same time the same application for the restoration of her sight, and this also she has now completely recovered. We have submitted a notification of the cure to Dr. Baines, our bishop. The person thus wonderfully cured is living in this neighbourhood and is ready to testify the truth of what I have told you. Lord and Lady Arundell, myself and others, are witnesses of it; and so we have every reason to give thanks to Almighty God for this signal instance of His goodness in reward for the faith of His afflicted servant. I remain, etc.

R. Parker.

from *The Life of Saint Winefride* (1922)

Eliseg
John Cowper Powys

In the Corwen churchyard, half-a-mile from our group of model cottages, stands a strange old pillar about a thousand years old, carved in the manner I have learnt from the writings of Massingham to link up — though this particular one is said to resemble some in Mercia — with the sacred pillars connected with the cult of the Earth-Mother in Crete.

Within an easy afternoon's bus-ride from where I live there is a yet more ancient pillar, bearing a defaced record to the effect that it commemorates the personality of a certain king of these parts called Eliseg, whose domains must have included, not only the umbrageous Dee valley, but the bulk of the pastoral uplands of Powys.

This monument to King Eliseg stands on a burial-mound within a few hundred yards of the ruins of Valle Crucis Abbey and never — not even at Glastonbury — have I felt the spirit of what Spengler would call the Spring-time of our Faustian Culture as powerfully as in this holy ground. The Thirteenth century Cistercian chapter-house remains entirely intact, and it would be easily possible to make use of this scholastic sanctuary in the mountains not only for Tibetan contemplation but for the writing of books.

from *Obstinate Cymric* (1947)

A Well Preserved Corpse
William Roscoe

The little hamlet of Llanrhaiadr, stands upon a slight eminence, about four miles from Denbigh. The interesting church and churchyard still detain the lingering foot of the traveller for many an hour. The east window of the sacred edifice contains a beautiful specimen of stained glass. The subject of the painting is the Root of Jesse, and represents the genealogical tree, springing from the loins of the patriarch, and comprising all the kings of Israel and Judah, encircled by branches and embowered in foliage, till the advent of the Saviour. A splendid full-length recumbent figure of Humphrey Jones, in full court dress, sculptured in white marble, lies on the left of the chancel. Monuments, containing the records of antiquity, rear themselves on every side in the churchyard, particularly one to the memory of John ab Robert, which descends through an infinity of abs from Cadvant, an ancient prince of Powis Land. I must not omit one, however, to the memory of Anne the wife of Edward Parry, to which appertains a most marvellous story. This pious female had opened her house for the preaching of the Methodists in this place, and originated a Sunday school in a neighbouring village, which she energetically maintained by her personal exertions. She ended a life of laborious benevolence by a peaceful death, and, forty-three years after her decease, on the occasion of her son's burial in the same tomb, from some circumstances her coffin was opened, and the body of this excellent woman was found to be in a perfect state of preservation, undecayed in the slightest degree, and her countenance bearing the hues of living health. The very flowers which had been strewed upon her body, it is said, were as fresh in colour, and as fragrant in odour, as when they were first plucked from their native stems.

from *Wanderings and Excursions in North Wales* (1853)

The Problems of Flintshire Priests
C.R. Williams

Few Flintshire parishes had a resident rector. Most churches were left in the care of a vicar. In many parishes there was no resident rector because the income of the parish had been given to the cathedral at St. Asaph or to Basingwerk Abbey. In such cases the canons of the cathedral or the monks of the abbey used most of the money for the benefit of the cathedral or monastery and provided a vicar. There was no rector of Llanasa, for example, because the income of this parish was used to provide lights and to repair the stone-work in St. Asaph cathedral. The income of Holywell church was used by Basingwerk Abbey. Another practice was to give the income of a parish to a student to enable him to carry on his studies at Oxford, or some foreign university. The rectories of Hawarden, Ysceifiog and Hanmer were used for many years to provide scholarships for students.

Because of these practices the parish clergy in Flintshire were usually very poorly paid. In Mold, Holywell and Llanasa the vicars were well-paid and received between £8 and £10 a year, but these were exceptions. In many cases the priests were little better off than labourers. Well-educated priests were, therefore, not attracted to Flintshire. A few had attended Oxford University and had obtained a Bachelor of Arts degree, which entitled them to be called 'Sir' (e.g. Sir Ithel, Vicar of Northop), but most of them had only attended the cathedral school, where they had learnt just enough Latin to be able to carry out the services. Yet, in spite of their lack of education — Archbishop Peckham said he had never seen such illiterate priests as in the diocese of St. Asaph — the parish clergymen were usually well-liked by their parishioners.

from *Flintshire from Earliest Times to the Act of Union* (1961)

Ffynnon Fair
S. Baring Gould

There is a holy well, Ffynnon Fair, in the parish of Cefn, in a beautiful situation, once very famous, but the chapel is in ruins, though the spring flows merrily still. It was the 'Gretna Green' of the district, for here clandestine marriages were wont to take place celebrated by one of the vicars choral of the cathedral, till all such marriages were put a stop to by the Act of Lord Hardwicke in 1753. The chapel was of the fifteenth century, and is now over-grown with ivy and in a clump of trees. Mrs. Hemans made this, 'Our Lady's Well,' the subject of one of her poems.

from *A Book of North Wales* (1903)

Persecution
William Williams

Thomas Lloyd of Denbigh was the owner of the house in which he lived, and because he made it a house of God, he incurred the displeasure of his persecuting neighbours. They could not turn him out of his habitation, but they seized all his furniture, leaving him nothing but the bare walls, and sold it publicly in the market-place. The same thing was done with the furniture of a house near Wrexham, where religious services were held. Every stick was taken to the town and publicly sold, and the whole of the proceeds was spent in drink. It was sport to some of the magnates of those days to plunge innocent families in the deepest distress, and to make their little property afford to the ruffianly tools of their despotism the means necessary for a 'jollification'.

Possibly all this was done under colour of law, and nothing was more easy. Complaint was made to a magistrate that a certain person held a 'conventicle'; the offender was heavily fined, and the rest followed as a matter of course. We could greatly multiply instances of this nature, but it would be a mere repetition to do so. Let it suffice to say, that this kind of oppression was allowed to go on for many years over a large portion of the Principality.

from *Welsh Calvinistic Methodism* (1884)

Revivalism
J.J. Morgan

The Mayor of Denbigh declared publicly on February 13 that the magistrates had only been troubled for over three months with one case, and he a strange tramp. In little more than that space of time 614 converts had been enrolled, 254 in Capel Mawr alone.

In a society one morning at *Saron*, in the Vale of Clwyd, two non-professing farmers were observed. 'We are delighted to see Mr. So-and-so here,' said the leader. 'I came by mistake; I thought it was a prayer-meeting,' said the farmer referred to, picking up his hat and leaving hastily. 'Was it by mistake *you* came?' the other was asked. 'Yes, really,' he replied; 'but if I may stay with you, I will.' He was welcomed, becoming an excellent Christian; the other was only embittered and further and finally alienated by his own unfortunate mistake.

As the lightning cometh out of the east, and shineth even unto the west, so came the power of '59 to Abergele. It was a Sabbath morning, and Joseph Evans, Denbigh, a young preacher, frail and wan, was present. His intensity of spirit was remarkable, and, too soon, the sharp sword wore out the fragile sheath. In the church meeting he rose to speak about the Revival. 'It will come to Abergele,' he declared. 'It is abroad in our land. It will come. *Oh* ! HERE IT HAS COME!' With these words, while his bluc-veined, attenuated hands were thrown up with a gesture of exulting welcome, a rushing sound like that of a fresh, strong breeze passed through the chapel.

Mr. Edward Roberts, C.M. deacon at Abergele, said that he had heard the same sound on two other occasions, both memorable in the story of Calvinistic Methodism. Once at Liverpool, in a great missionary meeting, Morgan Howells, Newport, rose to speak, and his first words were:

> O'er those gloomy hills of darkness,
> Look, my soul, *be still*, and gaze —

At the words 'be still,' a rustling sound traversed the large building, filling every bosom with alarm and awe, and making it necessary for the Rev. Henry Rees to intervene to quell the ensuing commotion. On the other occasion, William Roberts, Amlwch, that burning and shining light, was preaching on the field at Carnarvon Association. He was describing the Christian's 'abundant entrance' into the heavenly kingdom. 'O my friends!' he cried, 'you have had a life of toil and trial on earth; but your first glimpse of heaven *at the entrance* —' The sentence was broken short by a rustling wave of sound which seemed to strike and agitate the whole throng on the field. How can these things be? 'There are more things in earth and heaven than are dreamt of in our philosophy.'

One of the most fiery of the Revival preachers in the county was William Jones, *Talywaun*. It was his sermon on 'A feast of fat things, full of marrow,' that kindled the flame at Moriah. 'Another *dish* for you, my friends,' he would cry with every new point. The morning service lasted till one, the audience relishing the old preacher's dishes so much that dinner was forgotten.

from *The '59 Revival in Wales*, 1909.

Principles of Government
Daniel Owen

It would be impossible to write the history of Welsh rural life in this century without the church and the chapel featuring prominently in it, and anyone doing so would simply reveal his total ignorance. Remember that I am referring to this century. Where can one turn in Wales, however sparse and scattered the population, without finding a chapel belonging to one or other of the religious denominations? Usually it is a very plain building of four walls, a roof, a few windows and a door. If the locality is an old established community, one will probably find a grey old church with its melancholy old yew trees in the cemetery where many generations have been buried according to the evidence on the grave stones, which themselves more often than not now lie askew as if stricken by paralysis. These stones bear inscriptions of Welsh poetry — some good and others indifferent. But even the latter demand respect when one remembers that the poets themselves now lie buried there with neither stone nor stanza to mark their resting place. I have a strange feeling that it is the graveyards that give sanctity to the church and not the church to the graveyards. However great my prejudice against the Church of England as I recall the worldliness of the bare-headed and white robed parsons, gabbling the beautifully worded prayers over the mortal remains of hundreds of those now sleeping peacefully beneath the grass, my heart softens towards them, and I would, were it in my power, forgive and canonise each one of them. Say what you will there is an atmosphere in these quiet old graveyards which unites mankind, and calls on us to humble ourselves before our Creator . . . .

I am surprised to find, in some places, many chapels belonging to the same denomination. There is a North Wales town where it is possible to reach in half an hour any one of four chapels belonging to the same denomination. Two of these chapels have recently amalgamated to enable the members to pay for the ministry. It can, however, be said in favour of these many small chapels in the same district that though they are struggling to live they offer an excellent opportunity for the creation of chapel officials. It has been known after an election of deacons at which John Jones, Blaen y Cwm, has failed to get elected, despite his long devotion to the cause, for the said John Jones to become aware of the desirability of having a place of worship near his own home for the many backsliders, living nearby. John Jones sets to with renewed vigour and with considerable success to arrange services in his own home. Soon it is found that the house is too small and a chapel must be built, where of course John Jones is made a deacon, a position he had failed to attain in the 'old chapel'. The Irish talk of Home Rule, and the English of 'Three acres, a cow, and a district council,' but Welsh nonconformity had practised the principles of government long before them.

from *Gwen Tomos* (1894), trans by T. Ceiriog Williams & E.R. Harries.

Chapel-going in Winter
Emyr Humphreys

It was hot inside the chapel. The pews were occupied by whole families who had come to chapel prepared to face bad weather. Their clothing would protect them on the journey home. The wind had been rising all through the evening service. Impetuous gusts raced around the stout square walls searching for a gap in the defences. But Siloam was built solidly of stone quarried from the same hillside on which it stood. In spite of its exposed position above the road which led down to the sheltered centre of the village, the chapel was nailed safely to the hillside. The congregation sat drowsy with comfort and security. At the back of the chapel, in its own corner, an old iron stove maintained its distant roar and its chimney threatened to turn from black to dull red. Iron railings three foot high surrounded the stove so that the heat machine rumbled as harmlessly as a savage animal inside a cage. The tall chapel windows were decently draped in drawn blinds of a faded green colour, but not the decorative circles of glass above them. These, like portholes in a diving bell, gave an awesome glimpse of the black hostile night. But they were so high up it was easy to ignore them.

Inside the warmth of the chapel the well-trimmed lamps burned steadily, refusing to flare or flicker and the smell of paraffin was so reassuring it took on something of the power of incense. In the pulpit Mr. Buckley was immaculately dressed. He could have been a perfect model for an ecclesiastical tailor who also catered for non-conformist ministers. His voice was not as effective as his appearance and from time to time he had to clear his throat. But the whole congregation was on his side and sympathised with him in his struggle against the opposition of the elements.

from *Flesh and Blood* (1974)

Wesley at Mold
John Wesley

WEDNESDAY, 2 MAY 1759. I rode over [from Chester] to Mold in Flintshire, about twelve miles from Chester. The sun was very hot and the wind very cold, but as the place they had chosen for me was exposed both to the sun and the wind, the one balanced the other. And notwithstanding the Chester races (which had drawn the rich away) and the market-day (which detained many of the poor), we had a multitude of people, the serious part of whom soon influenced the rest, so that all but two or three remained uncovered and kneeled down as soon as I began to pray.

Journal

Religious Awakening In Buckley
Dennis Griffiths

Brickworks or chapel, or both, played a most important part in the formative period of our lives. Chapel meant much more than the place where we went on Sundays. We were taught that it came first in almost everything, so great was mother's insistence upon our loyalties being trained to that idea. Before I could walk there, I was carried both to chapel and to Sunday School, which I attended every Sunday morning. Chapel services were held on Sunday afternoon and evening in those times, and despite the embitterments which existed, a few men and women attended chapel in the afternoon and church in the evening. My two eldest brothers and my sisters also attended the week-night meetings, Prayer Meeting on Monday night, Christian Endeavour on Tuesday, and when sporadic enthusiasms of a somewhat fleeting character led to the formation of a Bible Class, or of another attempt to revive the chapel choir, they would be there, too. The visit of an itinerant evangelist or of a famous preacher occasioned great excitement, and when a few years later the Welsh revival took place, I remember that our chapel people were borne on the crest of an emotional surge little short of frenzy, and while it lasted, for seven nights a week they had services and prayer-meetings.

Whilst I was too young to join in these meetings, even a boy could not escape the fervour which swept through the principality at that time, when The Glory Song and Throw out the Lifeline could be heard at any hour of day or night. Then, as quickly as it came, the fever passed, and life resumed its normal pace. Not quite, for the Revival left folk floundering and breathless, unwilling to accept its passing now that they were denied the excitement it provoked. I remember too, how happenings during the Revival were now surveyed with a more balanced detachment. A few zealots who had found satisfaction and enjoyment in going to the penitent form night after night and being converted and re-converted, in meeting after meeting, chapel after chapel, now regained their former habits, some of them not so very laudable, whilst the story of one local preacher who was so transported in spirit that he actually started to climb up the stovepipe on his way to heaven went quickly round the town. It was at a revival meeting that the minister asked my sister, then fourteen, 'Will you come to Jesus, Annie?' 'I don't know,' she replied, 'but I'll ask my mother.' Even when she was a child, Annie was quite a realist.

Several families, mostly farmers, came regularly to chapel by trap, stabling their horses in the adjoining buildings during service, and of them, Mrs. Lindsay's family continued to the last. A Scotch family who came to live near Buckley, they were regular members. 'Kind people and good supporters of the chapel' was how mother would refer to them, and I also remember her telling me that when a match-making mother aspired to get Mrs. Lindsay's help to have her daughter engaged to an eligible local bachelor, she received the brisk reply, 'I've got corn of my own to grind'.

About the part the brickworks played in our lives, I will write later, but not a day passes even now without some little incident or other bringing back to my mind either the works or chapel of those days, incidents so small and unimportant that one wonders how memory has stored them. Was it the pathos surrounding that incident of a little sparrow which I saw one bitterly cold winter morning, deliberately committing suicide by walking into the blazing brickworks' kiln-fire, which causes me to recall to-day that simple little tragedy of more than fifty years ago? And was it because of too great a preoccupation for any child with thoughts of chapel that I had recurring nightmares about being locked-up there overnight, all alone? Actually, one little chap did have that experience after falling asleep during evening service. Fortunately, his frantic cries and blows on the thick plateglass windows with his little fists were heard by a passing collier on the way to night-shift, and the tearful little fellow, terrified by his experience, was released.

Then there was that awful fear of tumbling down from the gallery to the floor of the chapel, and even now I awake after dreaming that the wooden 'wall' which surrounded the gallery has sagged away, and I am either suspended in mid-air or crashing down to the seats below.

Vivid among these memories are those of many well-known characters whom I saw there, Sunday after Sunday. One of them was a portly, good-natured cattle dealer who snored in a deep, bass register throughout the sermon. Another, who, a 'strong man in prayer' as the old people used to say, left for Holyhead after service, travelling by train from Chester every Sunday night to buy cattle there at the Monday Fair. Another man, one of the several successful Buckley kiln-builders, had lost his teeth, but would suck peppermints with such energy that, with closed mouth, his jaws would work round and round, then up and down in a routine which was the nearest thing to perpetual motion I had seen.

from *Out of This Clay* (1960)

Folklore

Witches, Ghosts, Fairies, Giants
Sir Henry Morton Stanley

Mothers of the present day will understand how hard it is for a child of four or five years old to remain awake long after sunset, and that it was cruel ignorance on the part of Sarah to keep me up until ten o'clock every night, to listen to her prosy stories of ghosts and graves. Sarah's description of a devil, a curious creature with horns on his head, with hoofed feet and a long tail, was wont to make me shiver with fright. She was equally graphic and minute in her descriptions of witches, ghosts, fairies, giants and dwarfs, kidnappers and hobgoblins, bugaboos, and other terrific monsters, against whose extraordinary powers it behoved me to be always on guard. The dark night was especially haunted by them, and the ingle-nook by a bright fire was then the safest place for children.

If the grown folk had not all shared Sarah's belief in these gruesome creatures, I might perhaps have doubted they existed; but I remember to have seen them huddle closer to the fire, look warily over their shoulders at the shadows, as though they lay in wait for a casual bit of darkness to pounce upon them and carry them off to the ghostly limbo. Had Sarah but known how pain impresses the memory of a child, it is probable that she would have put me to bed rather than have taken me with her, as a witness of her folly and ignorant credulity. She believed herself to be very level-headed, and, indeed, by her acquaintances she was esteemed as a sensible and clever woman; but, as she infected me with many silly fears, I am now inclined to believe that both she and her neighbours were sadly deficient in common-sense.

One effect of these interminable ghost-stories was visible one evening when I went to fetch some water from the Castle well. It appeared to me that I saw on this occasion a tall, black spectre, standing astride of the Castle well. I took it at first to be the shadow of a tree, but tracing it upward I saw a man's head which seemed to reach the sky. I gazed at it a short time, unable to move or cry out; then the phantom seemed to be advancing upon me, fear put wings to my feet, and I turned and ran, screaming, and never once halted until I had found a safe hiding-place under my bed. The dreadful vision of that ghost haunted me for years, and for a long time I made it a rule not to retire until I had looked under the bed, lest, when asleep, ghosts and kidnappers might come and carry me off. The belief that the darkness was infested by evil agencies and ferocious visitants hostile to little boys I owe to Sarah's silly garrulity at Castle Row.

from *Autobiography* (ed. Dorothy Stanley 1909)

The Conjuror's Revenge
A.G. Bradley

Upon the high road once more, and heading for St. Asaph, we turn to the right, within a mile, at the old village of Henllan, which is chiefly famous for the tower and the body of its church being wholly independent of each other, and leading a separate existence. Anyone, however, with a fondness for folk-lore and witchcraft would do well to take note of the humble tavern here; for, according to the Rev. Elias Owen it was once the scene of a most marvellous and indeed humorous performance on the part of a local conjuror. The conjurors, I ought to say, were the witch doctors; but they sometimes did business on their own account, and in Wales were accustomed to assume at times most weird and fanciful attire. A high cap of sheepskin, for instance, with a plume of pigeon feathers, a gaudy coat decorated with talismanic charms, was the official costume of a gentleman who in bygone days worked wonders around Llanarmon. Like the Druids of old, and afterwards the saints, and finally the parsons of the earlier Church, the still more modern conjurors were, in a measure, hereditary. The seventh son of a family of sons could, if he chose, be the happy progenitor of a tribe of conjurors. The descendants of those who had eaten eagle's flesh were also born under the same mystic star.

But to our particular conjuror, who in comparatively modern times, while upon his way from St. Asaph to Pentre Voelas, stopped for refreshment at the same Henllan tavern. He partook, it seems, of ale and bread-and-cheese, but considered the price charged — sixpence for one and fourpence for the other — as outrageous. Like George Borrow, however, this medicine-man did not think it worth while to dispute a tavern bill, but he had a much more effective method of taking the change out of his hosts, so, paying what was demanded, he slipped a piece of folded paper under the leg of the table and went on his way. No sooner had the servant-maid entered the room to remove the empty jug and glasses, than a strange thing happened, for she began to dance as fast as her feet would allow her, singing at the same time (in Welsh, it is presumed)

> Six and four are ten, count it o'er again,
> Six and four are ten, count it o'er again.

The landlord and his wife, who were upstairs, heard the noise with astonishment, which was turned to wrath, in the farmer's case, when, descending to the parlour, he saw his maid-servant pursuing her mad dance regardless of his presence or his objurgations. Running forward with a view to knocking sense into the crazy girl, the moment his feet touched the floor the good man went off himself upon the same wild career, and there were now two of them dancing as fast as their legs would let them and singing with ceaseless refrain 'Six and four are ten, count it o'er again! Six and four are ten, count it o'er again'.

The old lady in the meantime was listening on the top of the stairs, and she could not credit her ears. She was not long, we may be sure, in descending, and when she got to the door, and beheld her husband and the maid flinging themselves about in this godless, demoniacal fashion, we can well believe the storm of indignation that rose within her matronly breast. What would have happened to her husband, if she had reached him, it is ill saying, but the moment she was over the lintel there were three maniacs instead of two making the dust fly and all shouting to the rhythm of their feet: 'Six and four are ten, count it over again'. This was a pretty state of affairs, but the babel soon brought the neighbours in, and one of them, sharper than the rest, remembered to have seen the witch doctor leave the house. His was the spell that had turned this sober household into a crew of maniacs, beyond a doubt, and he alone could undo it. So a messenger was sent full speed upon his track, and returned in a happily short space of time with directions to remove a piece of paper they would find under the leg of the table. This done, the breathless and exhausted trio were at last relieved from their involuntary gambols, and perhaps reconsidered their prices for a jug of ale and a crust of bread and cheese.

from *Highways and Byways of North Wales*, (1898)

Miss Jones and the Kippernappers
Gerard Manley Hopkins

Feb. 7. I asked Miss Jones in my Welsh lesson the Welsh for *fairy*, for we were translating Cinderella. She told me *cipenaper* (or perhaps *cipernaper, Anglice kippernapper*): the word is nothing but *kidnapper*, moulded, according to their fashion, to give it a Welsh etymology, as she said, from *cipiol* to snatch, to whisk away. However in corning to an understanding between ourselves what fairies (she says *fairess* by the way for a she-fairy) and kippernappers were, on my describing them as little people 'that high', she told me quite simply that she had seen them. It was on or near the Holywell road (she indicated the spot). She was going to her grandfather's farm on the hill, not far from where Justice Williams lived, on the slope of the Rhuallt. It was a busy time, haymaking I think. She was going up at five o'clock in the morning, when she saw three little boys of about four years old wearing little frock coats and odd little caps running and dancing before her, taking hands and going round, then going further, still dancing and always corning together, she said. She would take no notice of them but went on to the house and there told them what she had seen and wondered that children could be out so early. 'Why she has seen the kippernappers' her grandmother said to her son, Susannah Jones' father.

Journal (1875)

The Ghost of Pribwll
W. Bezant Lowe

Looking from the Chwibren side of the valley of the Aled, people were often in the habit of seeing a wheel of fire rolling with great force down the slope from Pribwll, and disappearing at the bottom. The explanation is supposed to be as follows: About a hundred years ago, there lived at Pribwll farm a man named Thomas; he was a cattle-dealer, and used to go to England to sell his cattle, and, as he was coming back one time with a large sum of money in his pocket, he suddenly disappeared. He was seen riding through the village on a white pony, and soon afterwards, the white pony was seen grazing in the fields of Pen Cefn Aled, but riderless. Thomas's relatives concluded that the man had been killed for the sake of the money he had in his pocket, and that he had been buried in the bottom of the valley, where the wheel of fire stopped.

A stone was to be seen in the old house of Pribwll, with spots of blood on it. Though it had been washed and rubbed, no one could remove the blood. It was the colour of the stone that in the first instance gave rise to the tale.

from *Llansannan: its History and Associations* (1915)

Saint George in Clwyd

W.T. Palmer

The Welsh claim that not only did George (a saint of the Eastern Mediterranean, adopted by the Crusaders) come to Wales, but that he performed (or repeated) his memorable exploit there. At the village of St. George in Denbighshire, which is claimed to have been the actual spot where he slew the dragon, they will proudly show you the hoof-mark of the saint's horse on the coping-stone of the churchyard wall.

The legend-teller in the inglenook is always apologetic about St. George and his dragon. In the vale of Clwyd the Welsh folk are notoriously without enterprise. How the Irish, Breton, Spaniard, would have revelled in a village of St. George, a legendary reptile, and the pious archdeacon who recorded that the deep dent in the church yard coping was made by a hoof in the great scrimmage! The occasion demands embroidery.

Elsewhere in Wales they revere St. George. Yes, indeed! Did he not rescue St. David from a magic thrall? Yet in Clwyd the story teller fails to piece together the important facts. Probably he thinks that the name of Magic in his vale is unconstitutional. He is wrong. If he sat an hour in April's glitter on Moel Fammau, when the air is clearing after a blizzard across the hills, he would know that his home is either a Garden of Eden at the least, or something too seductive in beauty to be quite honest . . .

from *More Odd Corners in North Wales* (1944)

The Tan-yr-Ogo Witch

J.O. Halliwell

On a rock to the westward of Abergele, high above the road, after passing the large modern castellated Gwrych Castle, is a singular cavern termed Cefn Ogo, the entrance of which has not been inaptly compared to the portal of a noble cathedral, arched, and divided within what has the appearance of a great column. This cave never seems to have been thoroughly explored. It is said to be penetrable about forty yards, when further progress is arrested by a chasm or by water, I could not with certainty ascertain which. The entrance is dirty and unpromising, and the large stalactites with which it abounds are neither fanciful nor brilliant. It is strange that no adventurous Welshman has yet penetrated the depths of this cavern, in defiance of the witch, who, according to local tradition, guards a vast treasure of gold at the very extremity of the cave. This is an absurd story told in the Month's Tour in North Wales to the affect that four men who attempted to explore the cavern penetrated to a distance that required the consumption of three pounds of candles, and that two of the company were lost in its recesses.

from *Notes on Family Excursions in North Wales* (1860)

A Notorious Well

Jan Morris

There were several well-known cursing wells in Wales, and of these the most notorious was the well of Elian near Llanelian-yn-Rhos in Clwyd. How this once saintly place acquired its evil nobody knows, but from the Middle Ages until the nineteenth century, perhaps later, it remained a centre of malediction. It stood in a corner of a field above a ditch, well away from the parish church on the higher ground above, and you can still see the faint track across the grass left by supplicants moving from the place of God to the place of mumbo-jumbo. The rivalry was direct. The well had its own self-ordained priest, and its forms, rituals and not least charges, like those of the church above, were established by centuries of usage.

If you wished to cast a curse a guardian would write it on a piece of paper and throw it into the well, and generations of rogues made a living from the practice. In the end the church authorities desperately arranged for the well to be filled in, and it was stoppered like a genie's bottle in 1929: but though it certainly seems sufficiently blocked now, and is surrounded too by a barbed-wire fence, hung with shreds of sheep's wool, still an unmistakably baleful sensation surrounds the place, as though evil effluences may still be escaping from it, and seeping into the muddy ground around.

from *The Matter of Wales* (1984)

An Ingenious Way to Kill Dragons
Marie Trevelyan

In North Wales a place called Llanrhaiadr-yn-Mochnant was associated with a dragon, or winged serpent, which went forth through a large district, and not only destroyed whole flocks and herds, but thought little of capturing men, women and children. Many plans were devised for the destruction of this monster, but without avail. By-and-by one man, wiser than the inhabitants of the district, suggested a curious arrangement. A large stone pillar was built and studded with sharp spikes of iron. As the colour red allures a dragon or serpent as well as a bull, the post or pillar was 'cunningly' draped with scarlet cloth, so that the spikes were carefully concealed. When the dragon next came forth, he was allured by the red drapery, and at once rushed towards it. The colour caused the infuriated creature to beat itself against the pillar for many hours, with the result that it died from exhaustion and loss of blood. The spot where the man-eating dragon beat itself to death is called Post Coch, or Post-y-Wiber, of Maen Hir-y-Maes-Mochnant to this day. The district frequented by this dragon, or winged serpent, is in the extreme south of Denbighshire, on the River Rhayadr, which forms the highest waterfall in Wales. The cataract of Rhayadr descends a rock over 210 feet in depth, and the river below marks the boundary between the counties of Denbigh and Montgomery.

from *Folk-lore and Folk Stories of Wales* (1909)

Sir John and the Dragon
W.T. Palmer

Here's another dragon story of the Vale of Clwyd, which is not often repeated. Incidentally it explains how Denbigh obtained its name. A terrible winged serpent haunted the precincts of the Castle of Caled-fryn-yn-Rhos, attacking man and beast till every one was scared away, and the town became almost desolate.

At last Sir John-of-the-Thumbs (so called because he had eight fingers and two thumbs on each hand), a member of the noble family of Salusbury, volunteered to attack the monstrous reptile. In the desperate conflict that ensued, Sir John succeeded at last in thrusting his sword deep under the dragon's wing, upon which, with a horrible yell, it expired.

Sir John cut off the monster's head, and bore it in triumph to the town where the delighted people hailed him with the cry, 'Dim Bych' ('No more dragon') — memorable words which in time passed into the place-name of Denbigh.

from *More Odd Corners in North Wales* (1944)

Sir Richard and 'The Evil One'
A. G. Bradley

Bachegraig, of which only one side of what was once a square is left, was the wonder of the age. Pennant in the last century saw the house still in its completeness, and says it rose into six wonderful stories, forming the figure of a pyramid, and was covered with much painted glass and quaint devices. The country people held firmly to the belief that Satan had supplied the materials every night for the next day's work, the clay for the bricks being dug out of the bottomless pit, and baked in infernal fires. Sir Richard, after its completion, was supposed to retire every night to a windowless room near the roof, for the purpose of conferring with the Evil One. This, was altogether too much for his wife's curiosity, which eventually overcame her discretion, for at length, unable to any longer contain herself, she stole upstairs upon tiptoe to the mysterious chamber, and there, peeping through the keyhole, sure enough she espied the nameless one hob-nobbing in most friendly fashion with her husband. But his Satanic Majesty's senses were far too acute for even the subtle Catherine's tactics, and, seizing Sir Richard in his arms, he burst with a wild yell through the brick wall, shattering the masonry in every direction. All this is to be accounted for by the fact that Sir Richard was a zealous astronomer, and had an observatory on the roof.

from *Highways and Byways in North Wales*, (1898)

May Eve and May Day Customs
Elias Owen

May Eve was, within the memory of the living, a busy night, for during the small hours after midnight young men were actively employed in letting the fair sex know the extent of their affection for them. If a young lady had jilted or discountenanced a suitor, then he had his revenge by fixing *Penglogau*, or skull bones, or dead sheep, to the house door of the lady who had rejected his advances; on the other hand the accepted happy swain dressed his sweetheart's door with flowers. Very anxiously did the fair await the dawn of morning, and happy were they if on opening the door they were greeted by a lover's nosegay, but very dejected and irate were they if dangling bones or a man of straw met their eye. This custom was common in most parts of North Wales.

Young men engaged in the uncongenial work of hanging skull bones at young ladies' doors were occasionally punished for their ungallant action by qualms of conscience, and their over-wrought imaginations conjured up phantoms which greatly disturbed their minds, and terribly frightened them. It is by such a supposition as the preceding that the following tale, told me by the Rev. John Williams, is to be accounted for. Mr. Williams states that he knew a respectable yeoman who told him that he and a companion were once going down the road from Derwen to Melin-y-Llwyn, having been out on May Eve fixing Penglogau at Derwen, when the yeoman observed a man descending the hill before them, carrying on his shoulder a large tree in full foliage, which he threw over the bridge with a great splash into the river Clwyd. His companion did not see the apparition, which immediately vanished, but he heard the splash. But this was not to be wondered at, for it is said that only those born under certain planets can see spirits, whilst noises which they make are audible to ordinary mortals.

Reference has been made to the festivities of May Day, but as the subject is in itself interesting, I will add to what I have already said, a few further particulars about the day. Aged people, born in the last century, often spoke with pleasure of the manner in which May Day was observed in their youth. In Abergele, it was a custom on May Eve for young men to go to Plas-uchaf wood, and bring thence a birch tree, which they planted on the Cross, a place so called in Abergele, where, probably, a cross once stood; this tree they decorated, and on May Day all the town danced around the birch May tree. It would seem that the ancient Welsh associated birch with love, and lovers formerly wore a birch hat, or *Het fedw.*

The Abergele May Dancers carried with them a *Cangen Haf*, or summer branch, dressed with valuable articles, and they were always accompanied by a *Cadi*, a man dressed in women's clothes, representing a busybody, who interfered with household affairs, and one of their number was a clown, grotesquely dressed in a fringed petticoat or kilt, who played all manner of antics. The May Dancers' music was not always to be despised. Not many years ago the youth of Flintshire and Denbighshire danced from new to old May Day.

On *Nos Wyl Ifan yn yr Haf*, St. John the Baptist's Eve, our ancestors dressed their houses, and washed or bathed their feet with *Llysiau Ifan*, St John's wort.

from *Old Stone Crosses of the Vale of Clwyd* (1886)

The Widow of Penley
Ken Radford

During the seventeenth century there lived in Flintshire a widow called Anne Ellis, who was known throughout the county for her vindictive ways and her skill in the art of witchcraft. She spent her days begging, and knitting stockings which she sold to the villagers. And seldom did anyone dare send her from the door. So afraid were they of her mischievous spells that they treated her generously and took care to give no offence, for those who roused her anger were stricken with misfortune. One deponent writes:

> when the sayd Anne is displeased she doth hurte to them and theirs, and further I can not say ...

On a winter's morning she was sent away hungry from the house of one John Byrch of Overton Forren. But before nightfall he was to regret his surly humour, for suddenly his daughter was taken sick. Suspecting that the child was bewitched, he sought out the widow in her wanderings and demanded that she return with him to bless the girl. For four days the spiteful woman refused to break the spell, and the child continued to suffer. It is recorded that:

> ... the sayd childe fell sike uppon Sunday night, and uppon Munday morneing ther appeared under the left arm a great lump of the bignesse of a hen's egg, the childe continueing in great paine, crying and lying uppon her face trembling ...

The following deposition gives further evidence of the mischievous wiles and vengeful ways of the widow, Anne Ellis:

> The examination of Elizabeth Jeffreys of Penly, in the county of Flint, taken by Andrew Ellise, esquire, one of the justices of the said county, uppon the theird day of June 1657, conserneing Anne Ellis suspect of witchcraft.
>
> Sworne sayth that about two yeares last past June the daughter of the examinant was very sicke and she feareing because of the reporte that the sayd Anne Ellis, of Penley, had done harme to the sonne of Elizabeth Taylor, aforesaid that the sayd Anne might alsoe have done hurte to her daughter, this examinant therefore went to the house of the sayd Anne Ellis and requested her to come see her daughter that lay sicke.
>
> The sayd Anne came and blessed the childe and shortly after the childe recovered, as is knowne to all the neighbours. This examinant sayth that about a month after the recovery of the childe shee was talking with the sayd Anne Ellis conserneing the same. The sayd Anne replied shee could goe to them and put any desease uppon any one.
>
> Not long after, this examinant's sayd childe fell sicke againe in the same manner beeing taken with a swelling all over her body and beeing soe deseased the sayd childe toulde her mother that it was allwayes soe when this examinant fell out

with the sayd Anne Ellis and that her sayd daughter dyed of the same distemper aboute Whitsunday the twelvemonth last past.

The examinant further sayth that on Saturday last past Margaret, the daughter of William Hughes, of Penley, came with other children to the house of the sayd Anne and did eate some of her bread in the abscence of the sayd Anne, whereat when shee returned home shee was extreame angry. Wheruppon this examinant desired the sayd Anne not to curse the sayd children nor to do them any hurte, whereat the sayd Anne made noe answere but muttered to her selfe.

This examinant sayth that when the sayd Anne is displeased shee doth hurte, that this examinant uppon Munday morneing heareing the sayd Margaret Hughes was fallen sicke, brought the sayd Anne to the house of the sayd Hughes to see the childe, who was sicke indeed, and the sayd Anne entred the chamber where the childe was sicke in bedd and put her hand on the childe and asked 'How doest thou?' She replied 'Very sicke'. Then the sayd Anne, putting her hand uppon the childe sayd 'God blesse thee, thou shalt mend after this'.

And further savth that shee hath heard an ill report of her the sayd Anne eight yeares and received her into her house more for feare than love, that when shee taxed her for curseing Richard Hughes afforesayd who hath bine a cripple this eight yeares suspected to be hurte by her, the sayd Anne replied asking why he did pisse downe her chimney ...

It is recorded that in the summer of 1657 Anne Ellis was committed to the common gaol, but cunningly made an escape from the constable. No-one knows what became of her afterwards; but it is likely that she spent the rest of her days preying on the superstitions of simple folk.

from *Tales of North Wales* (1982)

A Welsh Robin Hood
Anon.

Passing through beautiful scenery, I came to the old road which led to Denbigh through Rhyd Galed and Groes. As I stood looking about me, I saw a man crossing a field towards the road. He presently reached me, stopped and smiled. 'Good afternoon,' he said pleasantly. Then, making a few appropriate remarks about the weather, he went on, 'I hope you'll enjoy your holiday here. I saw you when I was in the village this morning, and was told that you were a visitor at the Saracen's Head.'

I thanked him, and then said in Welsh 'I'm glad you came along. I was just now wishing for someone I could ask a question or two'.

He seemed pleased when I spoke to him in Welsh, and he answered me in the same language.

'What is it that you'd like to know ?' he asked. 'I shall be glad to answer you if I can.'

'I believe there's an old tumulus near here somewhere called Robin Hood's Grave,' I said. 'I'd be grateful if you could tell me how to get to it.'

'It's quite close at hand,' he replied, 'but nothing remains of it now. Come with me and I'll show you.'

He led me to the other side of the road, almost opposite the lane along which I had come from Brynrhydyrarian. There in a field called Ffrith Wal Nesaf belonging to Deunant Isaf Farm, he showed me the site of the old tumulus, which lay close to the road and some fifty yards from the north-west hedge of the field.

'Who was this Robin Hood?' I presently inquired. 'The tumulus can hardly refer to the famous outlaw who roamed Sherwood Forest in the twelfth or thirteenth century.'

'The old inhabitants of Llansannan say that this Robin Hood was a Welsh chieftain,' he replied. 'On one occasion the English penetrated into these parts and were met by Robin and his men.' Here he paused for a moment, and pointing in an easterly direction, continued, 'Some mile or so yonder is a treacherous tract of marshy land. This marsh Robin caused to be covered with foliage in semblance of a pleasant grove, and on the other side of it concealed his men. The enemy was stationed a short distance away in the place since known as Rhiw Cyfrwyau, or The Hill of Saddles, from the circumstance that on that day the English saddles were strewn about on the slopes of the hill. Robin and his men made a clamour on the other side of the grove, which enticed the English to launch an attack, but instead of reaching their objective they found themselves sunk in the marsh, quite at the mercy of the Welsh archers. Those of the enemy who had not entered the marsh hastily mounted their saddle-less horses, and were pursued by Robin as far as where Bylchau Church now stands, some mile and a half away, in a southerly direction. Here the skirmish was continued, but resulted in the English being utterly vanquished.

South of the church is a field called Hen Fynwent, next to the field adjoining the church, which is supposed to have been the burial place of those slain in battle that day.'

from *A Vistor's Impressions of Llansannan* (1932)

Visitations of Death
Frederick J. Harris

Among the many superstitions concerning Death were the 'Canwyll Corph', or corpse candle, a ghostly light that was seen flickering when the death of someone in the village was imminent; and Cwn Annwn, a gang of spectral hounds that rushed past the wayfarer over the lonely moors on a moonless night in full cry after an invisible quarry. Another ghostly visitation, was the 'Tolaeth', or spectral funeral. A wayfarer at night would hear a loud chanting of Welsh funeral hymns, the sobs and groans of the mourners, and the tramp of the procession. Then would appear the singers with their mouths open, as in the act of singing, the coffin borne by four men, the long train of friends and neighbours usual in Welsh funerals, all passing by in deathly silence, for no one could both hear and see the Tolaeth. They could hear its approach, but immediately it came in sight all sounds died away.

from *The Welsh Elizabethans* (1924)

Death and the Spirits
Robert Parry

1589: This year in this country was seen many apparitions and walking spirits, by which sights and conferences with the same spirits many were brought to their graves. Many also died in despair, blaspheming and foretelling the like to others . . . such is the iniquity of our time that it is like that mercy will be turned to Justice if we repent not of our sins in time.

Many also died suddenly with little or no sickness and some without any sickness at all.

Diary

Acknowledgements

Every attempt has been made to obtain permission to include the items preceding: in some cases it has not been possible to establish the identity of the copyright owners.

The publisher gratefully makes the following acknowledgements:

For 'An Old lady', to John Idris Jones.

For 'Africa?' 'The Scholarship Boy' and 'An Urban Impact' by Emlyn Williams, to the Literary Executers of the Estate of Emlyn Williams.

For 'Farmland', 'New spaces, Clwyd' and 'Downing', to John Davies.

For 'A Walk Through Darkness' and 'Shaman', to Glenda Beagan.

For 'Gwytherin' by Ellis Peters, to Macmillan General publishing.

For 'Coastal Erosion', to Sue Trevlyan-Jones.

For 'Rhyl Sands', an extract from 'Autobiography' in *Collected Poems 1967-85* (Allison & Busby, 1986), © Adrian Henri.

For 'Today', to Bryan Aspden.

For 'The Glass Island', 'Wet Spring Bank Holiday, Dee Estuary', 'Pontnewydd Cave, Valley of the Elwy', 'The Dornier', to Gladys Mary Coles and Headland Press.

For 'An Estuary View', 'Pastoral', 'County School Pride', 'Twenty-four Pairs of Socks' Chapel-going in Winter' and his translation of Kate Roberts, 'Struggle', to Emyr Humphreys.

For 'Rhosllanerchrugog' and 'A Village of Colliers' by Raymond Edwards, to Gomer Press.

For 'At Valle Crucis Abbey' by A.G. Prys-Jones, to the Estate of A.G. Prys-Jones.

Acknowledgements

For 'A Wonder of the Age' and 'A Notorious Well' by Jan Morris, to Oxford University Press.

For 'Erddig Restored' by Merlin Waterson, to Routledge, Kegan & Paul.

For 'The Still Lake' and 'Bits and Pieces' by Euros Bowen, to Gomer Press.

'The Welsh Type' by Beatrix Potter: Copyright © Frederick Warne & Co., 1966

'Many Miles Astray' and 'The Llanabba Silver Band' by Evelyn Waugh are reprinted by permission of the Peters Fraser & Dunlop Group Ltd.

For his translations of Gutun Owain and John Ceiriog Hughes from *Welsh Verse* (Seren), to Tony Conran.

For 'Mystic Enchantment' and 'Eliseg' by John Cowper Powys, to the Estate of John Cowper Powys.

For 'An Indelible Mark on the Soul' by David Jones, to the Estate of David Jones.

For 'Dirty Williams' and 'Thinking of the Dead' by Robert Graves, to Carcanet Press Ltd.

For 'The Ecclesiastical Tour' by Ronnie Know-Mawer, to Souvenir Press.

For 'The Privilege' by T. Gwynn Jones, to Gomer Press.

For 'Philip Yorke, the Last Squire of Erddig' by Adam Mars-Jones, to Faber & Faber Ltd.

For 'Jones' by H.G. Wells, to The Literary Executors of the Estate of H.G. Wells.

'Drowning in Wales' by Philip Rock from *The Passing Bells* reproduced by permission of Hodder & Stoughton Ltd.

For 'Fishing on the Clwyd' from *Scouse Mouse* (Weidenfeld & Nicholson, (1984) © George Melly.

For 'Inside Denbigh Asylum' by Caradog Pritchard, to The Estate of Caradog Pritchard.

For 'The Bronze Age in Denbighshire', to Dr. Frances Lynch.

For his translation of 'Three Hinds of Denbighshire' and 'A Plea to Sir Bribem' and 'The Caerwys Eisteddfod', to The Estate of Gwyn Williams.

For 'Dispute and Conflict' by Trevor Hebert from *People and Protest: Wales 1815-1880*, to University of Wales Press/ Open University Press.

For 'Explosive Times' from *Hearthstones in the Hills* by Stowers Johnson, to Robert Hale Ltd.

For 'Stigmata' from *Clay Hill* (Poetry Wales Press), to Tim Liardet.

For 'The Grinding' by I.D. Hooson, to Gee & Son (Denbigh) Ltd.

For 'Misrule, Towyn, 1990' from *Selected Poems* (Seren), to Steve Griffiths.

For 'At the Eisteddfod' by Dylan Thomas from *Quite Early One Morning*, to J.M. Dent Ltd.

For 'Gaining Cheap Admission' by Cecil Price, to the University of Wales Press.

For 'Theatr Clwyd' by T.M. Haydn Rees, to Theatr Clwyd.

For 'Music in the Cathedral', to Raymond Renowden.

For 'Ferocious Honesty' by Kate Roberts, translated by Derec Llwyd Morgan, to the University of Wales Press.

For 'Reflections' by Kate Roberts, translated by Joseph Clancy, to the University of Wales Press

Acknowledgements

For 'Llanrhaeadr-ym-Mochnant', to R.S. Thomas.

For 'The Problems of Flintshire Priests' by C.R. Williams, to Gee & Son (Denbigh) Ltd.

The Editor

Dewi Roberts has spent almost all his life in Clwyd and its previous mainfestations. His keen interest in local history and in the literature of Wales are widely evident in this anthology, his second published book. A reviewer and essayist for a number of periodicals and journals, his first book was *Visitors Delight* (1992).